PRINCIPLES OF PRACTICE

BY PRINCIPAL SOCIAL WORKERS

To order our books please go to our website www.criticalpublishing.com or contact our distributor Ingram Publisher Services, telephone 01752 202301 or email IPSUK.orders@ingramcontent.com. Details of bulk order discounts can be found at www.criticalpublishing.com/delivery-information.

Our titles are also available in electronic format: for individual use via our website and for libraries and other institutions from all the major ebook platforms.

PRINCIPLES
OF PRACTICE

BY PRINCIPAL
SOCIAL WORKERS

EDITED BY
TANYA MOORE

First published in 2023 by Critical Publishing Ltd

British Library Cataloguing in Publication Data
A CIP record for this book is available from the British Library

ISBN: 978-1-915080-95-0

This book is also available in the following ebook formats:
EPUB ISBN: 978-1-915080-96-7
Adobe ebook: 978-1-915080-97-4

Cover and text design by Out of House Ltd
Project management by Newgen Publishing UK
Printed and bound in Great Britain by 4edge, Essex

Critical Publishing
3 Connaught Road
St Albans
AL3 5RX

www.criticalpublishing.com

Printed on FSC accredited paper

This book is for all the social work friends and colleagues who have inspired me over the years. We are all determined to be the best we can be.

Particular thanks to Shantel, Mark and Glory for advice and support.

And to James, Alex and Louie for love and green tea xxx

All royalties from this book will be going to Social Workers Without Borders.

Social Workers Without Borders is a social work organisation formed by volunteer social workers cross the UK, that uses our professional voices, skills and knowledge to defend and promote fairness and equality for individuals, families and communities who are impacted by immigration controls. Our vision is for a society where people's self-determination and welfare is not restricted by immigration policy and control. We believe that anyone who needs it should have access to support from social workers who understand immigration policy and who advocate for peoples' rights and freedoms. There are three strands to our work: campaigning, direct work and education. SWWB campaigns to promote and protect the rights of people with insecure immigration status and to challenge immigration policies that cause hardship, discrimination and injustice. Our 'Direct work' group undertakes and writes expert reports to support peoples' applications to remain in the UK or to be reunited with their families. We supervise a network of volunteer social workers to conduct independent social work assessments that are legal-aid funded or free of charge for people who cannot pay for this essential expert evidence. Through our 'Education group', we share this expert knowledge with the social work sector to support improvements in education and practice.

To become involved, please visit www.socialworkerswithoutborders.org

Contents

Meet the editor   page ix

Meet the contributors   page xi

Foreword
Lord Patel   page xv

Foreword
Ian Lawrence   page xvii

Introduction
Tanya Moore   page 1

Chapter 1
The patchwork of relationships
Sarah Range   page 7

Chapter 2
Ways of Writing
Fiona Hayward   page 15

Chapter 3
Relationship-based practice
Claudia Megele   page 23

Chapter 4
Relationships and Reciprocity? Strengths-based social work
in adult social care
Tanya Moore   page 33

Chapter 5
Safeguarding adults
Fran Leddra   page 45

Chapter 6
A reflection on online relationships and the changing landscape of practice
Claudia Megele   page 55

Chapter 7
Human rights and social work
Hannah Scaife   page 71

Chapter 8
Does sustainability have a place in social work?
Tendai Murowe   page 83

Chapter 9
Poverty and the need for radical relational practice
Lisa Aldridge   page 95

Chapter 10
Anti-racist leadership
Sara Taylor   page 103

Chapter 11
Understanding racial dynamics in supervision
Godfred Boahen   page 115

Chapter 12
Social worker's relationship with CPD
Tanya Moore   page 129

Chapter 13
Our well-being
Leire Agirre   page 137

Index   page 147

Meet the editor

Dr Tanya Moore has been working in social work and social care for more than 30 years as a practitioner, educator and practice leader. She currently leads on the professional doctorate in social work and social care at the Tavistock and Portman NHS Foundation Trust and was previously Principal Social Worker in Hertfordshire Adult Care Services. Tanya co-edited *The Anti-Racist Social Worker* (2021) with Glory Simango. Her research is on continuing professional development for social workers.

Meet the contributors

Leire Agirre

Leire currently works as the Head of Safeguarding, Quality Improvement and Principal Social Worker (Adult Services) in Central Bedfordshire Council. She has worked in health and social care for the past 27, starting as a carer in a care home when she moved to live in the UK. Prior to studying social work, Leire focused her academic interest in social policy and worked in varied operational and strategic roles across adult social care, the NHS, mental health services and the independent sector. Within her current social work leadership role, and as the chair of the Eastern Region Principal Social Worker network, she works to promote the well-being and safety of adults and has a keen interest in the notion and development of workforce well-being as one of the core pillars to great practice in adult social care services. Leire is committed to the importance of adult social care reform as a key opportunity to improve the experience of people in contact with adult social care, as well of those working within it.

Lisa Aldridge

Lisa has 22 years' experience in social work including 14 years at a management level. She has worked within Coram Family as a charitable service and within children and families services across the boroughs of Islington, Camden, Royal Borough of Kensington and Chelsea and London Borough of Hackney. Lisa has been employed as Head of Service for Safeguarding and Quality Assurance since 2016. This role has provided her with an excellent opportunity to develop her knowledge and skills in leadership while ensuring oversight of safeguarding and practice development in working with children across the children and families service as a whole. She has completed the Centre for Systemic Social Work Practice Leaders course and is currently undertaking her Professional Doctorate in Advanced Practice.

Dr Godfred Boahen

Godfrey is Principal Social Worker (PSW) and Head of Practice Innovation and Workforce Capabilities, London Borough of Hackney. His responsibilities include leading Hackney's preparation for the 2023 Care Quality Commission local authority assurance, implementation of Liberty Protection Safeguards and embedding of anti-racist in professional practice. Dr Boahen was the Policy, Research and Practice Improvement Lead at BASW (2017-20), where he led on the development of national practice frameworks on learning disability, autism and 'digital capabilities' in social work practice.

Fiona Hayward

Fiona has been a social worker for over 20 years, having studied at Southampton University following a four-month stint on an Israeli Kibbutz, which turned into five-and-a-half-year adventure. Fiona has worked in a variety of local authorities, as well as the private sector in her early career and has experience of adult and children's social services in different roles. Fiona has worked for Wiltshire since 2008 and is currently serving as Principal Social Worker which she describes as her dream job – promoting best practice and celebrating the profession.

Fran Leddra

Fran has over 30 years' experience in social care, with 17 years in senior leadership positions. As the Former Chair of the PSW national network and Chief Social Worker for England, Fran has represented social work at a national level, championing good safeguarding and strength-based practice. Now an independent consultant, Fran continues to promote good social work practice and provides mentoring support to PSWs.

Claudia Megele

Claudia is an authority in safeguarding and relationship-based practice and has held multiple leadership roles nationally and in local authorities. She has been a pioneer in digital practice in social work and is Fellow of National Institute for Health Research (NIHR), School for Social Care Research (SSCR); her research interests and expertise include digital safeguarding and the impact of technology on relationship-based practice. Claudia has published her work and research in multiple articles and books. Her books include: *Psychosocial and Relationship Based Practice*; *Safeguarding Children and Young People Online*; and *Social Media and Social Work: Implications and Opportunities for Practice.*

Tendai Murowe

Tendai has been a social worker for 20 years and has worked in child protection in the UK and Australia. She is currently working as Assistant Director for Quality Assurance in a London borough and was previously Principal Social Worker in Hertfordshire Children's Services. Her research was on the implementation of environmental sustainability in children's services, taking into account how important sustainability concerns are for young people. Her passion is in improvement, as well as providing excellent and sustainable services to children and families.

Sarah Range

Sarah started her career a care worker, moving on to qualify and practise in the US before emigrating to the UK. She has proudly worked for the same local authority for over 20 years. Sarah is the current Co-Chair of the National Principal Social Worker Network and has keen interests in the national footprint of social work, focusing on staff well-being and vicarious trauma, learning and development and legal practice. She is delighted work be part of this project with such esteemed and talented colleagues. Sarah is eternally grateful to her parents, her three siblings and E and N for their love and support.

Hannah Scaife

Hannah is the Principal Social Worker for Adults at South Gloucestershire Council and current Co-Chair of the Adult PSW Network. Since qualifying as a social worker in 2007, having worked for several years previously in therapeutic and residential settings with children, young people and families, she specialised in working with adults. She loves being a social worker – it is who she is, and she feels immensely privileged to have been able to be trusted, whether that is through direct work or as a social work leader, to build genuine, human, hope-filled relationships within which people can blossom and surprise themselves about what can be achieved.

Sara Taylor

Sara qualified as a social worker over 20 years ago and has worked since then in children's social care in various operational and strategic roles. She is currently the Head of Workforce Development and the Principal Social Worker in an inner London local authority. She has an MA in Social Work and Emotional Well-being. Sara is the Co-Chair of the London Region Principal Social Worker Network.

Foreword

Lord Patel

I believe that being a social worker is one of the most important and rewarding professions that anyone can do. I know that, like me, people become social workers because they want to make a real difference in people's lives.

Every day social workers are fulfilling complex and challenging roles and are using their skills and experience to ensure the protection of vulnerable children and adults. Social workers can, and do, transform lives for the better and I believe they provide an essential service for the people and communities they serve. The social work we practice is based in core values and ethical standards, which guide our actions and include the dignity and worth of individuals, integrity, competence and accountability.

We have a wealth of experience and knowledge within the social work sector and it is a pleasure to see it represented in this book, especially as critical reflections in practice are core to our professional development.

The essays in this book are significant as each chapter covers a different but essential facet of social work and provides us with much to reflect on and learn from. Each writer has spent many years in the social work sector and amassed a range of knowledge and experience. It also serves as a reminder of the strength and breadth of the leadership within the sector.

Most importantly, each writer reminds us that social work is not just about the learning of skills and models, but is about how we use them in practice, including the impact of our relationships and interactions, our influence on the world and environment, and how we effectively action change. The shared expertise of each writer provides a vital learning tool for all social workers to help grow and develop their own practice.

Above all, this book reminds us that social workers must never lose sight of the power we have to change lives. It's our responsibility to ensure that the people we work for and with have the ability to make informed decisions and choices for a positive impact on their lives.

Social work must continue to grow and develop, and books such as this can help us develop our thinking. It is only by reflecting on our practice that we can develop a profession able to adapt to emerging opportunities and challenges, build public trust and confidence in the profession and ensure that social work has a strong voice.

Kamlesh
Professor, Lord Patel of Bradford OBE

Foreword

Ian Lawrence

It's only when someone has influenced you by unwittingly and, often in the simplest of ways, tapping into your history, that the penny drops and you realise the importance of relationship and communication and connection. I didn't ask to develop a mental illness and I certainly didn't ask to be admitted to hospital but within that huge negative came human connection and learning.

Being human to one another is always the key to success. As social workers we can theorise about this and even build it into our processes but as a recipient of professional input I can confirm that it's often the unnoticed nuggets of humanity that make the most profound difference.

Social workers may feel pressure to take action, see impact and move onto the next person. But relationships don't work that way. My life was changed and my path reset by a small throwaway comment from a health care assistant on the ward where I was detained. *'I read you're a manager in social services,'* she said. *'You carry yourself like a manager, if you don't mind me saying.'*

This purely delivered statement showed this worker had taken the time to get to know a bit about me. I didn't know the impact her words would have upon me until some months later but, for me, this simple interaction seemed to validate my existence as a human. Her words reminded me of who I was before my life fell apart. We can know many theories and apply them effectively but, as this book suggests, behind it all is the core of simple humanity toward a fellow human.

This simple and short interaction made the difference between me being able to return to work or further sinking into despair. It gave me a small hope when I was hopeless and allowed me to take the leap of faith towards my own healing. Often, we don't recognise the impact of the relational elements of our practice. I let this lady know the difference she'd made to me and it was clear that she'd had no clue how important her words had been.

As a recipient of services, a carer and a social worker I'm aware that small can be beautiful. The processes I've experienced have left me frustrated and confused but having someone hold my hand when I was at my most vulnerable was validating and reassuring. This respectfully offered touch carried information about person to person connection. Without communicating such genuine warmth professionals won't get beyond my instinctive (and essential!) defences.

I'm excited about this book and hopeful for the thinking it will generate. I wish you all well in expressing beautiful relational connection within our professional social work practice.

Ian Lawrence
Ian blogs and tweets as The Samurai Social Worker
https://gusvassell.wordpress.com/
@SamuraiWorker
@positivesimply

INTRODUCTION

Tanya Moore

Social work is a relational practice. Social workers work within the context and container of relationships and reflect carefully on all there is to be learned from them. Conscious attention to empathetic connection is particular to social work and we know from people who use our services that this relational drive is key.

But we're busy. We're under so much pressure to get things done that we risk losing sight of the primary importance of this human connection. It's the role of Principal Social Workers (PSWs) to create balance between meeting demand and maintaining the standards essential for thoughtful, informed and personalised practice. There are PSWs in both adults and children's services and all are responsible for leading on social work practice within their authority. Some Children's PSWs use the title PCFSW (Principal Child and Families Social Worker), but for ease I'm using the term PSW to cover both adults' and children's roles.

The PSW role comes in different forms depending on the size of the local authority. Some PSWs work at team management level, others are placed higher up the management structure working as service heads or directors. Some have standalone PSW roles overseeing quality and direction of practice across the organisation. Others have hybrid roles that include responsibility for specific services. All function at the strategic level of the Professional Capabilities Framework for social workers, champion the rights of citizens using services and advise the Directors of Adult and Children's social care on practice matters. All are highly skilled and experienced social workers and leaders with a passionate belief in the power of practice to support people to get to where they want to be in life.

It's such passion that has led to the creation of this book. *Principles of Practice* sprang from an animated discussion between a small group of eastern region PSWs in a restaurant in King's Cross. We were in what we hoped would be the tail end of the Covid-19 pandemic and were discussing the different meanings of resilience to people using services, social workers and service providers. The dramatic improvement in online communication at the start of the pandemic had been a significant factor in our own resilience as it meant we'd been able to meet regularly, form a bond and share support. We'd found the local and national PSW online networks to be a rich source of insight and direction. We wondered at the vast amount of practice knowledge and experience held nationally at PSW level and struck upon the idea of a book to offer a wider platform for PSW thinking. We reached out to a small number of PSWs who we thought might be interested in writing for the book and put a note in the PSW newsletter inviting more. The ask was for current or former PSWs to write about an aspect of practice that's particularly important to them and the result is the plethora of practice principles you're about to read here.

Social work is multi-faceted and each chapter represents just one area of interest for the writer. Of course, PSWs have many practice passions and there are easily enough ideas for chapters to fill more books on practice principles. But however broad the topics presented here, the unifying theme is clear. Social work happens through relationships.

The chapters

Relational connection is the focus of Chapter 1, in which Sarah Range describes some of the key relationships from early in her career and reflects on the impact they've had upon her understanding of social work. If our practice is based upon relationships, she argues, social workers must be given the reflective space needed to process their emotional impact.

Relational practice extends beyond the time spent with people to the way we write about them; we know our written records have the power to cause distress and trauma either now or when people feel ready to look at their files in the future. Recording must be accurate but also sensitive and respectful. In Chapter 2, Fiona Hayward shares examples from Wiltshire's Ways of Writing project in which recording is completed with the child in mind meaning it is written as a letter that the child might read when they're older. Writing directly to the child offers a way of helping their future self make sense of what happened when they were younger and extends the power of the relationship with their social worker as a model for sensitivity, understanding and strengths-based thinking.

Good recording can be seen as evidence of relationship-based practice. As can the response of people to our attempts to connect. In Chapter 3, Claudia Megele presents the EMPOWER model of relationship-based practice. Co-created with 180 social workers, EMPOWER offers a series of questions to help social workers reflect upon the relational elements of our work and serves as a helpful reflective checklist for relationship-based practice.

But relational connection presents its own challenge. In Chapter 4, I argue that such challenge has led to the oversimplification of the powerful potential of strengths-based social work. True application of strengths approach creates relational vulnerability and I suggest that we may unconsciously protect ourselves from such vulnerability by locating strengths practice in the stable of 'positive psychology' approaches. I propose a new model of Relationships and Reciprocity in which relational connection remains the containing factor to strengths approach but there's capacity to acknowledge the painful presence of need for help and support while also responding to the shared need for two-way connection.

Relational practice recognises the importance of all relationships. In Chapter 5, Fran Leddra tells two stories from practice in which community connections enabled people to keep themselves safe. Both stories show the importance of acknowledging need for support as well as a will to contribute, and show that with genuine two-way connections people can develop a sense of safety and belonging. Good safeguarding practice, argues Fran, is often about knowing when social workers should step back and allow the power of the community to step up.

The seemingly unlimited scope of online community brings a different set of advantages and challenges. In Chapter 6, Claudia Megele extends her relational gaze to relationships formed on social media. The positive potential of online community connection was demonstrated during the Covid pandemic, but its anonymity and invisibility have created a different set of safeguarding considerations. Boundaries between work and home and online and offline presence have been significantly blurred, and Claudia highlights a need for a sophisticated grasp of e-professionalism for social workers.

Within our work, it's often the 'ordinary stuff', such as being called by our name or being able to see a dentist, that needs to be protected. Hannah Scaife presents the protection of such basic dignity as social justice and calls for social workers to stand alongside citizens to ensure rights aren't breached. In Chapter 7 on human rights and social justice, Hannah presents our role in noticing what matters and helping people gain and maintain control of their lives.

The major structural challenges to social justice are climate change, poverty and racism, and as social workers we must concern ourselves with all three. In the face of such oppressive forces, social work must organise a professional response at organisational, local and national level, but we must also take individual action to make the changes that are within our gift.

Tendai Murowe links poverty and environmental degradation to families' inability to keep their children safe. Tendai's research found a high level of environmental awareness among social workers, but climate change must be a professional as well as a personal issue for social workers and Tendai makes a clear connection between climate change and the immediate lives of the people we support. Chapter 8 demands that social workers take up the agency we have and lead the way on environmental responsibility.

In Chapter 9, Lisa Aldridge demands that we draw upon our radical social work roots and recognise poverty as an affront to human rights. Lisa challenges social workers completing assessments to be explicit about the causes and personal impact of poverty. Locating the Poverty Aware Social Work Paradigm firmly within the context of relationship-based practice, Lisa calls upon social workers to highlight the social injustice that leads to poverty and to stand in solidarity with the people most impacted.

I originally received five offers for chapters on anti-racism for this book but, for the sake of balance, took the difficult editorial decision to restrict this to two entries. Sara Taylor's chapter, Chapter 10, details her work to become an anti-racist leader. Using the *'Social GGRRAAACCEEESSS'* as a reference point, Sara explores her own position in relation to privilege and power and describes the steps taken by her organisation to open up awareness and dialogue and make purposeful moves towards becoming an anti-racist organisation.

In Chapter 11 Godfred Boahen examines racial dynamics in supervision and presents a table of how power manifests in supervision through the possible racial dyads, such as *'White supervisor, Black supervisee'* or *'Black supervisor, White Supervisee'*. Racial and power dynamics are present in all possible dyads, notes Godfred, even where both supervisor and supervisee identify as the same *'race'*. Godfred's table of supervision dyads should form the basis of every supervision agreement as it offers awareness of and ability to articulate the complex racial dynamics that must be noticed, named and examined if they are to be overcome.

Many local authorities have revised their training offer to ensure anti-racism features prominently and social workers have sought out further awareness and understanding through podcasts, reading and videos. This is an example of social workers making it our own business to develop our knowledge. Continuing professional development or CPD is a requirement of social work registration. It's not difficult to fulfil because social workers love CPD. But even CPD has an important relational element to consider. In Chapter 12, I suggest our relationship with CPD is likely to be heavily influenced by our original relationship with learning; if we were happy learning at school, we're likely to be happy learning now. But, just as when we were younger, learning was likely to have been easier if people around us took a supportive interest, so we can support each other's CPD by building an active interest in CPD into the life of our teams.

We should also consider how we can build social workers' well-being into the culture of our teams. In Chapter 13, Leire Agirre continues the animated King's Cross discussion by presenting resilience as an interaction between the worker, the workplace, the culture and the physical environment. Relational focus isn't just between social worker and client; it extends to the ways social workers look out for one another and look after ourselves.

CHAPTER 1

THE PATCHWORK OF RELATIONSHIPS

Sarah Range

For E and N. My eternal love and gratitude.
Mom and Dad — thank you for the gift x.

Introduction

Relationships are the bedrock of social work practice. In my role as a PSW, I'm uniquely placed within the authority to provide senior management support and represent the voice of social work practice across the organisation. But there's only one PSW in each department and it can get a little lonely, so it's important to make time to reflect on practice with peers. My chapter is the result of a series of conversations with a trusted peer; with my PSW colleague (and editor), Tanya Moore, I have reflected on some of the relationships formed throughout my career and have considered the emotional impact as well as the learning from each of them.

The patchwork of relationships

In our relationship-based profession, connections between people are the platform for change, but we need to be aware of the impact of these connections on ourselves as well as on the people we support. So it's important that our reflection should be upon both the impact we have on others and also our own emotional experience of the work. It's this acknowledgement of mutual impact and vulnerability that I consider to be the basis of relational social work. In this chapter, I re-visit some of the key relationships that have formed my approach to practice and from which I continue to learn today.

Core memories set the path

I distinctly remember the smell of the hospital. Stale air, scented with alcohol, shoe polish and crisp cotton. I remember as a small child, holding my mother's hand, stealing glances at those who passed in the hallway. The slightly dazed, excited new father rushing towards Maternity, or the older couple draped in the shock of unanticipated loss. I was taught not to stare, but to say a prayer that the nurse would know how to help them get better.

A long line of women – my mother, aunts and grandmother – all earned their crust healing and supporting the visitors to this hospital. My aunts were the linchpins of the Emergency Room, working swing shifts as Charge Nurses. In the post Roe vs Wade 1970s, these two powerhouses were confident and determined, leading with steely focus. Down the hall, my grandmother was secretary to the Chief of Emergency Services. My grandmother had the pulse of the hospital and assisted Dr G in ensuring people most in need received critical care. My mother was tied to this same hospital, through her training and early career as an X-ray technician.

The hospital was a consistent presence in the day-to-day life of my home where we were driven by co-ordinating shift patterns and sleep schedules. A strong Italian-Irish American family, it was customary for the adults to talk exuberantly about their jobs. For us, this meant animated discussions about injuries, illness and hospital politics. Perhaps it was easier to cope with a conversation about the illness itself rather than the distress and disruption it can cause.

The women in my family occupied their lives in the care and service of others and between them they impacted the lives of thousands of people. But it was their impact on me that set me on the path for my own career in social work.

Preparing for my turn

Early on in my time at university, my mother arranged for me to do a short placement alongside a psychiatric nurse. Aged 20, armed with my own white hospital housecoat, I joined the overnight vampire shift in the ER. The hospital was in a deprived inner-city area, known as a neutral zone between rival gangs. It had been chronically underfunded for decades and served a disenfranchised population where health inequalities were the norm and were played out between the buffering high-rises of affluence that encircled it.

One evening, the nurse I shadowed was called to three major incidents. The first involved a man who had attempted suicide by taking his wife's birth control pills. The panic and despair felt by his wife was immediately evident, but the nurse brought steadying order and process into the situation through quick assessment and negotiation of a plan. She arranged for the man to be seen by the Psychiatry Team for assessment and carefully explained options for support to him and his wife. Later, in supervision, I considered the apparent futility of attempted self-harm with hormone pills. But my supervisor challenged me to think more deeply about what had been communicated and reminded me of what his wife had said about how his depression seemed to have taken hold since the birth of their third child. It may be that on some unconscious level he'd been expressing a need to hold back the growth of his young family by taking contraceptive pills. Of course, this is just a hypothesis and couldn't be fully explored in the ER, but this man's experience showed me that things are seldom as they seem; we need to be alert to all forms of communication and interest and curiosity are key if we are to develop any meaningful understanding of people's experiences.

On our second call, we visited a cubicle where an emaciated man lay in the bed. He was tiny, dwarfed by the clinical whiteness of the hospital bed. This was the early 1990s, during the height of the AIDS epidemic, and this man was on his own. He was dying and he was scared. I vividly remember the conversation. My supervisor asked if he had any family members that she could call to be with him. He replied he couldn't contact his family as they didn't know he was gay and had AIDS. She tried to reassure him that it wouldn't matter to his loved ones, but he was racked with the isolation of an illness that lacked societal acceptance. He'd experienced the death of his partner to AIDS some months previously and he knew what the future held for him. I was floored that this man would die alone, and outraged and incredulous as to why he would choose this end without the comfort of the people who loved him. I began to understand how precious and yet how fragile the relationships that make up our lives can be.

In the early hours of the morning of that shift, the sleepy ER suddenly became electric, pulsating with police officers and chaos. A young man was rushed in by ambulance. He'd been involved in a gang shooting and had been left in front of the hospital with a gunshot wound in his chest. I felt my fear and adrenaline rise as this young guy was intubated by the attending physician. I could see the man was roughly my age and keenly felt this as a connection. Watching colleagues manage the most intense situation with deft command and control, I knew that although I was deeply impressed by the adrenaline-filled kindness and professionalism of the hospital staff, emergency response wasn't my calling; I wanted time to get to know and to support each of the people who had been admitted.

The pantry

My family danced precariously on the poverty line. Working-class, blue-collar American grit. My parents both had multiple jobs but there was always more week than money left at the end of a pay cheque. I spent my early years playing in the yard of my trailer home, surrounded by the woods. It was much later in life that I recognised myself as a walking caricature slur of poverty in the USA. Later, when my siblings were born, the economic crises of 1970s/80s America bit harder. As a teenager, I didn't understand why I couldn't have the latest Jordache jeans and embarrassment and shame were constant companions until, on the back of my parents' double shifts, scrimping, and sacrifice, I went off to university. I was the first person in my family to attain a college degree.

As part of my university programme, we had to arrange our own 40-day volunteer placement. I chose a local food pantry. Growing up poor, I understood food stamps, Grade A US Government Cheese, free school milk and the stigma of the public welfare system.

The food pantry was a hub of the neighbourhood. My job was to radiate warmth, trust and welcome and to normalise the experience for the people accessing the centre. The true beauty of the pantry was most evident in the stockroom and kitchen, staffed by volunteers who were a tapestry of helpful hands. Helpers interwove with those seeking help but all gravitated to the kitchen at lunchtime. Eating together was a leveller. It was here, listening and connecting with helpers and helped, that I learned that misplaced sympathy can be destructive; it can erode hope. What was required to make the food pantry a supportive environment were relationships based on equality, respect, honesty and trust.

The tapestry of the practitioner, relationships the thread

Later, as a newly qualified practitioner, I worked extensively with older people. The impact of the connections formed with people then have remained long after the deaths of the people involved. The vignettes below are of a small number of the people who have impacted me and my practice, through our shared vulnerability and connection.

Early in my career, I worked with a woman living in a sheltered housing complex for which I was the assigned social worker. The request was simple enough; at the age of 89 she felt she needed some support to clean her home. This lady had no children; her husband had died many years before and she lived by herself. We talked about her early life, her young womanhood and the excitement of her courtship and marriage. Suddenly, a deep sadness occluded her eyes, her composure changed and she was flooded with emotion. She told me she had become a mother but her baby had died. Her grief was raw and palpable and it overwhelmed us both. I learned that in the post-war 1920s, it was expected that her loss would be replaced by the birth of another child. This child sadly never came and the loss of her baby continued to haunt and cause fresh pain all these years later.

Reader, I cried with a client. For the most part, such apparent lack of containment is seen as taboo and my more experienced self might question the value and impact of a social worker responding to a situation by appearing to be emotionally overwhelmed. Yet still I look back and recall this to have been the right response. My tears didn't portray a lack of control; they showed an authentic emotional connection. This lady's experience didn't relate in any way to mine so I wasn't confusing my own story for hers, but I was responding to the profound sadness being presented. I cried with a mother, a woman who was once young, as I was then, in response to her gut-wrenching loss that grew in density as she reached the end of her life.

Years later, I still reflect upon and question my response to that woman's sadness. These days, I advocate emotional connection as a part of professional composure but there are very occasional instances where tears can be an appropriate acknowledgement of sadness. Of course, I don't mean uncontrollable sobbing, which is more likely to be a sign that the presenting sadness has triggered a personal source of pain. But with this lady who was alone with her grief, I hope my boundary-bending compassion was a comfort and a genuine communication that her grief had been understood.

Keys to connections and solutions

The rapid development of connection and trust provide the keys to connect people with solace and solutions. In this story, Daisy was the key. Daisy was the late wife of an older man with whom I worked. I can see his face as he sat in his chair, head back, lost in memories. In the course of our work, we'd talk about their life together, their adventures and the beauty and vivaciousness of his late wife. He told me he was struggling; his home was showing signs of his decline and he was falling frequently. But despite this, every night he'd sit and have a sherry with Daisy's memory to end their day. Being young, with not much experience about the world, I asked an innocent question ... how big was the glass? Turns out, the traditional toast of an evening had developed into a dependence equating to an 8oz full tumbler of sherry, every night! This was the cause of his deteriorating mobility and increasing falls. My genuine curiosity and the work we'd done to develop a connection of trust gave us a way in to helping him think about useful changes he could make to increase his social contact, reduce his loneliness and, ultimately, reduce his drinking. The wonder of the right questions, sown into a relationship rich with interest and trust, can provide the eureka moment to spark change.

But relationships create vulnerability in all participants, and for some people this can be too much to bear. Mr Z was in his 70s, and spent his days sitting in his kitchen, overlooking the street, and the car which he could no longer drive. I'd heard how 'difficult' he was from other workers; he was seen to be insulting, disparaging, unresponsive and dislikeable. I could understand these views. Case in point, always a person endowed with curves, Mr Z would call me 'a big girl' and comment on the size of my bottom. I now understand this rudeness as a tactic to make me keep my distance.

Aggression, discord and abuse permeated the key relationships in Mr Z's life. His military demons, broken relationships and his self-neglecting older years pushed people away and shaped his approach to connections. But I was determined to stay the course and, over time, our relationship broke through his usual patterns to establish roots. We worked together for the 18 months before his death, trying to improve his life, on his own terms. I visited him in the hospital at the end of his life. It was a scorching hot summer day and the ward was filled with drawn white curtains. Mr Z was heavily medicated and barely conscious, alone.

My mind snapped back to another man, this one so much younger and yet still dying alone behind a white curtain, without friends or family. Confronted with another lonely and undignified ending, I recognised the stark limitations of a professional relationship. The connections we offer are real and can have profound impact on all involved. But, as paid workers, there are limitations to our role and we can never replace the rich sustenance of a genuine connection that comes from shared family history, mutual enjoyment, combined interests or just that special spark. And this is how I continue to understand the boundaries of the social work relationship; it's not about holding back or behaving differently, it's a recognition that the most value comes from natural connection and our role is to see these are nurtured and developed.

Mr Z's death felt devastating. I drove to his funeral but couldn't bring myself to go in; instead, I sat outside and watched his small family file into the funeral home. It would have been easy for me to have been influenced by the labels applied to Mr Z by previous workers. But Mr Z wasn't 'unlikeable' or 'hard to engage'; his reluctance to connect with workers was driven by his lack of familiarity with warm relationships. He had been lonely and what was understood as bitterness was actually his self-protection. His defence tactics were successful in keeping unwanted emotions at bay but also in pushing people away. I've encountered this dynamic many times in the years since and consider it a function of social work to model healthy connections. But, in this instance, the experience of a positive relationship was sadly not enough. Mr Z was unable to reconnect with his family and, ultimately, he died alone.

Final reflections

Relationships are two-way and social workers are impacted by the relationships we form just as much as are the people we support. The unique element of a social work approach is that the connection between client and worker forms the springboard for change. If our professional relationships remain superficial, this is all that will be experienced and an opportunity for meaningful and helpful connection will have been lost. The need to maintain professional boundaries is not a licence for transactional practice which favours processes and systems over authentic connection, but with authentic connection comes vulnerability. If we're to make a personal investment in every person we meet, this has the potential of coming at a personal cost. There needs to be some protection built in for both client and worker and this takes the shape of an informed exploration and understanding of the impact of connection and a mindful, accountable and value-driven approach to its use. Either supervision or peer reflection can be ideal containers for this.

Whether we use individual or group supervision or whether we create reflective networks with trusted peers, if relationships are the bedrock of social work practice, then full professional attention and priority must be given to their impact.

Reflections

Reflecting on the learning from this chapter, consider the following three questions:

- How have previous connections and relationships shaped your values and beliefs?
- In what way do you bring your authentic self into practice?
- To what extent do you use supervision or peer reflection to explore the impact of the connections and relationships you form with the people you support?

CHAPTER 2

WAYS OF WRITING

Fiona Hayward

This is dedicated to all social workers past, present and future and to my sister, who without realising it was the subconscious reason I became one!

Introduction

Writing in children's social work seems to have gradually morphed into a rather strange combination of empty social work jargon and borrowed multi-agency lingo. Our clumsy use of language has hindered our ability to build relationships with families and children.

Several years ago, I read a letter written by a Child Protection Chair to a child after a case conference; it was powerful, direct and unlike any social work writing I had seen. The language used was respectful, clear and sensitive. Importantly, there were no acronyms, no jargon and you didn't need to be a social worker to understand it. I began to think about the impact of our recording on the young people who will later come to read their records and to question whether the way we write now would give them a clear view of their early life.

Shortly afterwards in 2019, TACT Fostering and Adoption published the ground-breaking guidance *Language that Cares: Changing the Way Professionals Talk About Children in Care*. Written in collaboration with children experiencing social care, it stated that the way we use language can create stigma and barriers. The guidance takes the form of a dictionary of terms preferred by children and young people. Wiltshire Local Authority, like a number of others, has been working to embrace the suggestions made by the young people with TACT and to develop an approach to recording that is inclusive, clear and respectful.

Our new Ways of Writing approach is heavily influenced by the TACT guidance. In our approach, we don't write *about* the child, we write directly *to* them and sometimes *with* them. Some practitioners describe it as writing *'in the moment'*. I think it's helpful to think of all our recording as a letter to the child. We write with the understanding that one day the child will read what we've written and the information we've recorded will form a significant part of their future memories and understanding of their earlier years. Just as photographs can fix moments in our memories, the words we use in our recording might fix recollections and understanding for young people in the future. They serve as a therapeutic way to fill in narrative gaps and explain decisions that were made at the time. Our words can build upon future perspective and confidence, or they can undermine or damage a young person's sense of self. We should choose and use our words with care and deliberation.

In this chapter, I will share some of the learning points we've gleaned under Ways of Writing and illustrate these points with examples of recording. The examples I share give an indication of how we are using the guidance in Wiltshire. They aren't actually taken from our files but are inspired by the approach to recording that has been adopted by social work and foster care professionals in Wiltshire.

Include names

We think it's important to always include names of people who have been in the young person's life. This helps to generate and maintain memories.

> *Your Year 5 teacher Mr Abioye has said that you are settling well into your new school and that you are working nicely at the Triangle table with Meena, Edie and Dillon.*

Be clear and factual

There may be no other source of information available to the young person, so our recording needs to be accurate and factual but not at all judgemental. There are many ways to understand the same situation and, while stating the facts, our recording should also offer an explanation that values the strength of the young person's relationships.

We are involved because we think that your dad needs some help to keep you safe. It's difficult for him to trust us and it's hard for him to keep to all the appointments we make. But because he wants to get things right for you, he has worked to cooperate with us and this is to his credit. I really hope he is able to continue with this.

Avoid generalisations

There's nuance to every situation and we try to accurately reflect this in our recording. So generalisations are to be avoided.

Your mum told me she finds it difficult to make new friends in the playground and other places because she's nervous to meet new people. Because of this, it was tricky for you both the first few times she took you into school. But for the past two weeks, she's been finding it much easier and has made friends with one of the other mums.

Help young people to understand their story

We try to describe complex emotions in an accepting way.

Sometimes you can feel a bit overwhelmed with worry. It's sad when this happens as it makes it difficult for you to concentrate, even on fun things. But the good news is that you are able to tell people you trust when you are feeling this way. And we can help you feel better by being extra kind and caring towards you. You always like us to be clear with you, and in return you are clear with us and this is really helpful. Sometimes, you like to have time on your own and you are very good at letting us know when this is the case.

Capture narratives

Continuity of interest helps build up a fuller picture of day-to-day life.

Your room was extra clean today! That's 5 days in a row. It was beautifully tidy and you had even emptied your bin! Fantastic!

Allow the child to come alive on the page

We like to include details both to give the reader a fuller picture of the child and to help the child connect with the life of their younger self.

I picked you up from Alex's house and we went out to Nando's for tea. You were so happy and excited. You were eager to leave the house and you were jumping up and down in excitement.

Capture and celebrate the lovely

Just as family members often like to repeat and celebrate young people's successes, so do we.

You had your second Covid jab today. You were very brave. The nurse gave you not one but three stickers because you liked them so much. Afterwards, we went for ice cream.

Write with empathy, sensitivity and respect

We think difficult emotions can be described in a respectful way.

It's my birthday and I remembered that sometimes, other people's birthdays can be really hard for you. We talked yesterday about how we wanted to make it a fun day for all of us. Then today, you gave me a lovely picture and a smelly soap. We went out for cake and although I think it was difficult for you when your brothers arrived, you remembered what we had talked about and you stayed calm. Thank you. I really enjoyed spending my special day with you.

Write in a sensitive, trauma-aware way

We try to write our care plans in a down-to-earth way.

> *We have agreed that on the mornings you are feeling worried about school, you will go in through main reception. If it would help to sit in Mrs O'Reilly's office for a few minutes, this would be fine.*

Write about concerns clearly and sensitively

One of the biggest practitioner worries at the start of this work was that risks to children would become minimised, but we think it's possible to state our concerns in a factual way that is clear but not negative.

> *There is a plan of things your mum and dad need to do keep you safe. This includes sorting out the garden. At the moment, there are broken tiles, overgrown thorns, broken garden furniture and an unsafe trampoline. When I visited today, I reminded your parents they needed to sort all this out.*

It is possible to analyse and think about risks while writing to the child:

> *There's lots that's going well but I'm still worried about you because your mum can often radiate towards friends and have relationships with men who can be dangerous and scary and this places you as a little child at significant risk.*

And to write about how barriers can be overcome:

> *Gloria Macdonald, our learning disabilities nurse, has been helping your mum learn how to attend to everyday things like cleaning your teeth and sorting out headlice. Your mum is determined to get this right for you and working with Gloria will give her the confidence she needs and will make you feel happier at home too.*

We think even very complex, worrying situations can be recorded sensitively.

> *Your sister is experiencing some health problems as a result of her drinking. This week, she's having some tests on her liver which was*

damaged when she was drinking before. Your sister was sober for a number of years and knows she can do this again. She really wants to make this work as she wants to continue looking after you but she'll need lots of help to manage the daily job of running a home. I am particularly concerned about you now though because when your sister has spells of mental ill health, she isn't always able to choose the best ways of managing and this can make things difficult, upsetting and unsafe for you.

Writing with a child or young person can be a helpful way to affirm messages and to help the child take some control over what is happening.

Your dad's friend took advantage of you. He's an adult and he understood that what he did was very wrong. He has been arrested by the police. You and I have talked about tomorrow's meeting where we will plan about how to keep you safe and support you. There will be your mum and dad as well as Mrs Jude, Raj, my manager and Ellie from the police. You have decided you don't want to come to any part of this meeting but that you're going to write a letter that you'd like me to read on your behalf.

Consistency

We believe that everyone who enters words into a child's file should adopt a consistent approach to recording. And being able to help a child understand their journey and the decision making throughout, the authorising manager will explain the reason for a decision, and might write the following:

We are worried about you because of a domestic abuse incident between your mum and dad and we think there should be a plan to make sure you stay safe and well cared for. We call this a 'child in need' plan. I think your parents have mostly managed to keep their difficulties from you but this can be hard for all concerned. I'm pleased to see that overall, you're doing well. You have good support from your family who love you very much and we don't think you are being seriously harmed, but I do think you need support while your parents get some help to make sure you are well and happy while they work out how to settle their relationship.

Writing to the child has had results we did not anticipate and we are recognising the power of our recording as a practice tool. The writing has enabled some families to shift their thinking. A social worker said of a pre-birth assessment she had addressed to the unborn baby:

> I read this aloud with the parents and they commented how powerful it was to hear the worries written down as if explaining them to the child. It helped them to understand impact and they were able to see life more clearly from their child's world and rather than feel guilty, were able to make changes.

Recognising the impact of trauma and stigma on parents, another social worker wrote sensitively with detail about interactions between a mother and her baby. Later, she said:

> I gave the case notes to a mother whose baby had been removed. The mother really liked reading about the positivity and warmth she had given her newborn and found comfort in knowing that her baby might one day read such positive, personal and warm notes that highlight the love and attention she was able to give in those early times. She thought her child would be able to know they were loved by their birth mother as a result.

Our Ways of Writing approach started as a way of ensuring children can understand their childhood narratives, know about the decisions that were made and help to fill potential gaps in childhood memories. We hoped it would also promote strengths, develop understanding of trauma and capture a detailed account of a family's life in a sensitive way that can help us to build and sustain relationships.

Paying more attention to what we say and what we write has had a far greater impact than we envisaged. It has helped families to see life from their child's perspective; to understand what can negatively impact on children. Detailed writing from childhood helps future relationships where we may be seeking to repair and heal. Our Ways of Writing approach has acted as a lightbulb moment for families and has shifted how we as practitioners communicate. Considering what we say and how we use language has profound effects on the families we work with – promoting strengths, understanding trauma and ultimately choosing language that builds and sustains relationships has the potential to change life courses.

Reflections

- If you haven't already, do look at the TACT guidance – the web address is given below.

- What memories of your own childhood are particularly important to you? How well might a young person access memories such as these from their case records?

- What steps can you take to ensure that young people supported by your service have access to a clear, respectful and sensitive record of their early involvement with social care?

Reference

TACT Fostering and Adoption (2019) *Language that Cares: Changing the Way Professionals Talk About Children in Care.* [online] Available at: www.tactcare.org.uk/content/uploads/2019/03/TACT-Language-that-cares-2019_online.pdf (accessed 21 November 2022).

CHAPTER 3

RELATIONSHIP-BASED PRACTICE

Claudia Megele

Introduction

A small boy called Ethan often ran away from school after lunch. His teachers felt that he was *'disruptive'*, didn't respect the school boundaries and labelled him as a *'trouble maker'*. Ethan was nervous at school, found schoolwork hard and didn't have many friends. He would spit at the other boys so no one would come close. He did this mostly because he felt scared of the other boys and preferred to be alone. His teachers and social worker said he was *'difficult to engage'*, *'unruly'* and *'purposefully isolated himself'*. When his teaching assistant went on maternity leave Ethan received support from a new teaching assistant (Lucy) who gradually was able to build a trusting relationship with him. Lucy didn't use language such as *'disruptive'* or *'difficult to engage'*. She spoke about adults needing to understand Ethan's perspective and what might be worrying him. She emphasised the things Ethan was good at. Lucy's language and her approach were very different from those of the other adults in Ethan's life and she began to form a positive relationship with Ethan. So one day when Lucy asked Ethan why he didn't want to stay in school after lunch, he wasn't sure why but he felt he could trust her and share his secret: *'My dad hits my mum and that's why I need to be home. I go home to protect her.'*

Ruth has lost almost everyone and most things in her life apart from her magazines, notebooks and pictures that remind her of a time when she had friends, a husband, children, love and laughter in her life. Ruth feels very lonely most of the time and only has the television and her magazines for company. Ruth isn't sure how it's happened but lately her house has become so full she can hardly move around the house to cook or wash herself. She had help from the council before; a very busy man called Paul came out and got her some help to clean her house. She started to feel worried, scared and lonely and before long there were large piles of things again around the house. Ruth would like to ring Paul and ask him for help, but she feels embarrassed as to what he will think of her, getting herself back into the same predicament again.

These two experiences highlight the importance of relationship-based practice. They also highlight that relationship-based practice is well distinguished by children and young people as well as adults, and although they may not be able to define it they are able to describe how it makes them feel. Relationship-based practice enables practitioners to better understand the experiences of the people they work with. This is because it offers the connection needed for people to feel safe enough to explore and express their thoughts even where it means sharing 'deep secrets' or overwhelming feelings. The preceding examples also highlight that, although as practitioners we can offer practical support, if that practical support isn't combined with good relationship-based practice at best it won't bring about lasting change and at worst it can perpetuate cycles of shame, blame and fear. So, let's briefly examine what makes relationship-based practice.

What is relationship-based practice and what is its significance?

From its inception, social work has been rooted in community and relationships. Good practice and effective interventions take place through empowering relationships that enhance people's well-being and aim to achieve greater equality, equity and social justice. Indeed, at its heart, social work has always been an enabling and empowering relationship-based practice. Therefore, contemporary relationship-based practice can be thought of as effective use of self and relationships to enhance people's life-journey, development, resilience and well-being. In this sense, relationship-based practice is a systemic and evidence-informed interdisciplinary approach to empowering relationships.

Recognising people's essential humanity and the importance of connection and community, social work considers people as being both subjective and social at the same time. Relationship-based practice takes place at the intersection between the individual's psychological/internal world and subjective states (eg happiness, sadness, depression, etc) and their social/external world and objective statuses (eg age, race, socio-economic status, unemployment, etc). Relationship-based practice requires an eclecticism that is interdisciplinary by nature, systemic in thinking and integrative in approach and practice (Megele, 2015, p 3; Megele and Buzzi, 2017). However, as Nigel Elliott (2017) says, such 'eclecticism can be misapplied amounting to no more than a random magpie way of doing things'. Instead, what is needed is a disciplined and flexible eclecticism, based on a reflective understanding and assessment of the context and matching the method to the situation and desired outcomes (Elliott, 2017, pp 335–9).

However, although building positive relationships with others is an important element of relationship-based practice, to think that relationship-based practice is limited to building good relationships with people who access services and is an end in itself, is to miss the point. Relationship-based practice requires a clear sense of purpose with a focus on positive outcomes and enhancing the person's well-being. Empowering relationship-based practice requires effective and purposeful use of self which in turn needs both self-awareness as well as other-awareness and a reflective application of theories, values and principles of social work in practice.

Each social work encounter is a relationship-based encounter involving all the complexity of navigating life's challenges and achieving greater growth, development and well-being. Indeed, a primary focus on process and procedures and a process/procedure-driven practice is often a psychological defence mechanism aimed at masking and somehow avoiding practice complexity and its uncertainties, anxieties and challenges. Relationship-based practice instead offers recognition and respect for individuals and their narratives and honours the autonomy, expertise and experiences of people in their entirety with all their complexity.

So, a holistic understanding and application of relationship-based practice is an essential prerequisite for effective and empowering social work practice.

EMPOWER: A helpful model for relationship-based practice?

A few years ago, a colleague and I asked practitioners for their views about relationship-based practice. This consultation with 180 practitioners led to the co-creation of a tool that highlights important elements of relationship-based practice. The EMPOWER reflective questioning model supports practitioners to think about their own practice in a critical and yet constructive manner. EMPOWER is an acronym and stands for Empathy, Motivation, Person-centred and purposeful, Observation, Whole-system, Empower, and Restorative and reflective approach.

These components are a good reminder of some of the central elements of relationship-based practice. They help us cultivate meaningful relationships and support people who access services to achieve positive change while promoting practitioners' creativity, autonomy and systemic thinking within a disciplined approach to ensure that direct work with children and families remains purposeful.

Empathy

Empathy is our ability to develop an understanding of another person's thoughts or feelings in a given situation from their own perspective. Empathy is different from sympathy in that empathy is about feeling with and alongside other people. Empathy generates the experience of shared thoughts and feelings which in turn foster trust, whereas in sympathy one is moved by the thoughts and feelings of another person and yet remains emotionally distant from them. Empathy sets the foundation for healthy and effective relationships. It creates a non-judgemental space that promotes self-expression and acceptance.

Empathy offers us the ability to understand another person's thoughts and feelings in a situation from their point of view, rather than our own. It differs from sympathy, where one is moved by the thoughts and feelings of another but maintains an emotional distance.

Ethan's experience and others demonstrate the importance of empathy and how our own professional anxiety can result in labelling and how this can make children invisible and their lives and experiences misunderstood in practice.

In contrast, empathy and a practitioner's non-judgemental acceptance offer the experience of being understood. This in turn fosters self-acceptance and trust in others.

Motivation

Although empathy and positive regard lay the foundation for better connection and relationships, without motivation we can't achieve positive change. Motivation is what moves people and makes them do what they do. In practice, we need to ask ourselves what are this person's motivations? Why are they doing what they're doing?

Motivation is a complex and multi-faceted phenomenon and although our understanding of motivation continues to evolve (Kanfer et al, 2008), it is evident that people are motivated by a wide range of factors. Understanding people's motivation offers better understanding of their actions, aspirations and intentions and enables practitioners to co-produce better and more sustainable change. However, people who experience trauma and/or significant and persistent difficulties and setbacks may end up losing hope in the possibility of change or a better alternative. So they may need help and support to regain their hope and confidence in life and its opportunities as well as their own capabilities and possibilities. It is by tapping into and harnessing people's motivations and the motivation to change that we can induce and achieve positive change.

Person-centred and purposeful

Person-centred is about putting the person at the centre of the service and all we do and ensuring their best interests by allowing them to take the lead in practice and tailoring solutions and interventions to their circumstances, identity, culture and preferences.

Being purposeful is about being outcome-focused and clear about the purpose of all that we do — eg the purpose of a home visit, assessment, communication or initiating statutory intervention. A purposeful person-centred approach requires that the goal of all interventions is aligned with the wishes and priorities of the people we work with; in this manner, a purposeful person-centred approach provides a balance for achieving positive change within the framework for social care services.

Being person-centred enables us to put people and their lived experience at the forefront of practice. It offers recognition and visibility to the voices, experiences, aspirations and preferences of people who access services and requires good observational skills and the ability to hold the role of the observer.

Observation

The role of the observer is both a privilege and a challenge, and the ability to hold the role of observer is essential for social work. However, the observer role requires a combination of skill and capacity that to a large extent can be learnt and developed.

Observation goes beyond seeing and requires being fully present and emotionally experiencing. It involves finding a distance close enough to experience the feelings involved in the other person's relationships but far enough to be able to think about them.

It is always interesting to see someone else's perspective and to note the similarities and differences between your observations and those of your colleagues or your peers. Indeed, you might find great differences between your observations and these always provide a good point for reflection and expanding our view and perspective.

Whole-system thinking and approach

A whole-system approach is about systemic thinking. In practice this means understanding the family as a system of relationships that operate within and interact with other systems such as schools, the parents' employment and workplace, community and social cultural systems and influences. Such understanding offers a more enriching and holistic approach to appreciating the experiences of the people we work with and the complexities of everyday practice. Therefore, as relationship-based practitioners with a whole-system approach, we consider all the interactions in people's lives and the different factors that impact experience and well-being.

Empower

When I ask social workers why they chose this profession, about 95 per cent say it's because they want to help others. Although this is a noble cause, we should not confuse helping with wanting to rescue people. Providing professional help and support is a privilege that entails great responsibility, can only be helpful when it is carried out within professional boundaries and is informed and led by the people we work with and leads to their greater empowerment.

Empowerment is about offering validation to people's experience and identity. This means respecting and honouring the views, preferences and motivations of the people we work with. Respecting the expertise people hold in their own lives, within professional boundaries and with an outcome-based focus, is an essential prerequisite for positive and sustainable change. After all, empowerment requires giving voice to people's thoughts, ideas and wishes and enabling them to reach out and achieve their desired self-narrative. Empowerment can only happen through an empathic, person-centred and purposeful relationship.

Restorative and reflective approach

In contrast to deficit-based approaches, the restorative approach builds on positives and enhances people's social capital. This is a relationship-based approach that can be adopted flexibly from a more informal to a more structured manner. This includes tapping into and developing people's connections and support networks in a safe and purposeful manner in a series of more or less structured meetings and activities.

Restorative practice seeks to remedy the trauma and harm experienced as well as the relationships that have been damaged. For example, rather than punishing an 'offender', restorative approach aims to build their awareness and responsibility for the consequences of their actions. One approach is through meeting with the people who have been affected by their and hearing about how they have been impacted. These meetings serve the dual purpose of reflection and learning for the 'offender' while giving voice and validation to those who have experienced the consequences of those actions and perhaps helping them to forgive and move on. In this sense such meetings offer an opportunity for learning, reparation and reconciliation between those involved.

Finally, reflection is at the heart of relationship-based practice and is a pre-requisite to empathy. The ability to see oneself and critically examine our own actions, emotions, thoughts, motivation and outcomes in the context of practice is foundational to our professional development and to effective relationship-based practice.

Self-supervision and the EMPOWER reflective questions: Some points of reflection when thinking about relationship-based practice

E – Empathy questions:

- How is this person feeling and why?

- How do I feel about this encounter and why?

- What do these feelings mean/reflect about the person's feelings, thoughts and lived experiences?

M – Motivation questions:

- What is the motivation behind this person's actions? And what does that tell me?

- What is the person's motivation for change and why? How can we develop a shared understanding of priorities?

- How can I support this person and enhance their motivation for change to enable them to achieve better outcomes for themselves?

P – Person-centred questions:

- What are this person's values, preferences and priorities? And what are their concerns?

- How do I ensure that all my actions and decisions are guided by this person's needs, rights, wishes and preferences?

Principles of Practice by Principal Social Workers

O – Observation questions:

- How can I maintain the role of the observer?
- What are some of the power differences and/or external factors that may influence my observation, relationship and interaction with this person? How can I mitigate these power differences and external factors as well as their impact?
- How do I maintain the role of the observer so I can learn more about this person's lived experience while being helpful and interacting with the person?

W – Whole-system questions:

- What is the context of this person's lived experience? And what are the contextual factors that are helpful or unhelpful for this person at this time?
- Who is in this person's social network and what is this person's social capital? How can I help enhance this person's social network and social capital?
- How would a given action, decision or change in this person's life influence the different aspects of this person's lived experience and well-being?

E – Empower questions:

- Are my actions, decisions and motivations in line with this person's preferences?
- Does my practice promote the voice of this person? Does it validate and give expression to the person's experience and identity?
- Does my practice meet this person's needs, rights, wishes and aspirations and does it enhance their well-being?

R – Restorative and reflective questions:

- Is my practice and language free from shame and blame words and approaches?
- Are my actions and decisions and practice focused on this person's strengths and how do they contribute to this person's development and well-being?
- How can I improve my practice and better support this person to achieve more positive outcomes?

Conclusion

From its inception social work has been rooted in relationships and community; even its name, 'social' work, reflects the social and relational dimension of this profession. Relationships and relationship-based practice are inseparable and foundational to good social work practice with adults and children. However, at times relationship-based practice is misunderstood and the EMPOWER questioning model offers a practical framework to think about relationship-based practice. EMPOWER's reflective questions are helpful reminders that offer a practical and yet critical lens for reflecting in and reflecting on practice and enhancing our own and others' experiences and life-journeys.

Reflections

- What are some of the factors that can help or hinder effective relationship-based practice?

- Think of an experience when you worked with children and young people or parents or adults who access services; how could you use the EMPOWER model in those circumstances?

- How can you use and apply the EMPOWER relationship-based model in your practice and your work with children and adults who access services?

References

Elliott, N (2017) Psychosocial and Relationship-based Practice. *Journal of Social Work Practice*, 33(3): 355–9. DOI: 10.1080/02650533.2017.1373083

Kanfer, R, Chen, G and Pritchard, R D (eds) (2008) *Work Motivation: Past, Present, and Future*. New York: Taylor & Francis Group.

Megele, C (2015) *Psychosocial and Relationship Based Practice*. Northwich: Critical Publishing.

Megele, C and Buzzi, P (2017) *Safeguarding Children and Young People Online*. Bristol: Policy Press.

CHAPTER 4

RELATIONSHIPS AND RECIPROCITY? STRENGTHS-BASED SOCIAL WORK IN ADULT SOCIAL CARE

Tanya Moore

Introduction

Strengths-based social work is seen to be accessible and positive but is also accused of being simplistic and superficial. In fact, it's a highly demanding way of working that engages fully with the difficulties of people's lives. In my chapter, I explore what it means to take a Strengths approach and consider how the term has come to be so misunderstood. I suggest a model of Relationships and Reciprocity to remind us that Strengths can only work as part of a relational connection. But the emotional connection required for an authentic Strengths approach demands commitment and vulnerability. To avoid a superficial application of a complex approach, I maintain that we need good reflective space to process our practice.

What is Strengths-based social work?

Strengths approach is a collaboration. One person tells their story and the other listens carefully, noticing the strengths and coping mechanisms embedded in the account. These are reflected back to the teller.

Strengths approach to social work was developed by social work academics at the University of Kansas in the 1980s and popularised in the 1990s by the publication of 'The Strengths Perspective in Social Work Practice' (Saleebey, 1996). It responds to the tendency of deficit-focused approaches to pathologise. It demands that we recognise people with whom we're working as equals, *'willing to meet them eye to eye and to engage in dialogue and a mutual sharing of knowledge, tools, concerns, aspirations, and respect'* (Saleebey, 1996, p 303). It's described as an expression of some of the deepest values of social work (Weick et al, 1989).

The accusation of superficiality stems from an oversimplistic understanding; Strengths does see hardship and messiness in life but it refuses to condemn people to a life of restriction or distress. Instead, it looks for the personal resiliencies that help people manage. It believes that challenges or mistakes can create growth.

Strengths-based conversations begin with open, affirmative questions such as *'what helps you cope?'* or *'what's most useful for you?'* but it takes attentive and empathetic listening for the teller to trust their story will be respectfully heard. And it takes focused attention for the listener to spot the hints of resilience that may be hidden under difficult experiences. Reflecting back resiliencies creates an important counter-narrative that can help the person locate their own coping mechanisms and begin thinking constructively about next steps.

Strengths practitioners are optimists who see potential for growth in everyone. This means they can be confident there will be always resilience to reflect. However, reflections must be genuine; fakes don't ring true and the approach can only work where there is trust.

Strengths approaches are not a panacea; they don't cure all problems and they don't work for everyone. But they can be an effective way to emphasise the person's agency; however difficult things have been up until now, the Strengths practitioner will spot ways the person can gain more control over their life.

Strengths approach is usually described in terms of its principles. These are:

- a belief that focus on deficiencies is not useful, so focus is instead upon strengths, resiliencies and coping mechanisms;

- optimism; everyone has the capacity to learn and grow and change;

- the collaborative partnership between person and social worker is key;

- the person is the director of the helping process;

- community is a source of potential support.

Strengths Approach and the Care Act 2014

The Care Act (Department of Health and Social Care, 2014) has steered our practice away from needs-led problem/solution approaches to prevention of escalating need by focusing on well-being. So instead of asking about difficulties, we're encouraged to have conversations about how people might live a life of reasonable comfort. Strengths approach is presented as a *'perfect framework'* (Department of Health and Social Care, 2019, p 50) for Care Act-compliant practice. It's been heavily promoted by the Chief Social Worker (Department of Health and Social Care, 2018) and features in both the Professional Framework for Social Workers (BASW, 2018) and Social Work England Professional Standards for social workers (Social Work England, 2019) as an expectation for practice in social work.

Does it work?

There isn't much evidence about the effectiveness of Strengths approach although this is probably a sign of how generally difficult it is to get watertight evidence about the effectiveness of social work interventions. People's lives are complex and there are so many variables that might impact the outcome that it's difficult to know for definite what has caused change. But we do know that practitioners say their practice is better because of Strengths approach (Nelson-Becker et al, 2020) and, interestingly, that newly qualified social workers seem to find the approach easier than some more experienced colleagues. This may be an indication of how much of a shift it is from traditional problem-based approaches. Used alongside human rights, person-centred and relational approaches, Strengths offers a steer away from conversations about what's wrong and an opportunity for the person and the people most important to them to be heard.

The problem with Strengths

Strengths approach might intuitively *feel* like a good idea but it can be undermined by its oversimplification and the lack of high-quality supporting evidence. It's misleading to present it as a simple and accessible approach and important to understand its complexities and pitfalls. Strengths has been accused of sanitising difficulties that are too great to acknowledge (Saleebey, 1996) and this is exemplified in the misguided opening question *'What are your strengths?'*. Richardson (2020) describes this question as *'reductionist'*. I add that it can

> simultaneously side-step the personally directed narrative which is essential to a strengths based conversation, dismiss the reality of the difficulty of the person's experience, shift the responsibility for identi-fication of strengths from the practitioner to the person and deny the power dynamic of the role of the social worker as gate keeper to ser-vices who will need to be persuaded that the person has need of social care support.
>
> (Moore, 2022, p 27)

This last issue is perhaps the biggest criticism from people needing help; Strengths approach is seen to underplay need and, if true, this would be counter-intuitive in the face of limited service availability, tightened eligibility criteria and a need to argue for entitlement to support.

Strengths approach isn't easy because difficulties tend to be complex. It's tempting to want to locate the problem with the person because individual problems are usually easier to fix than wider structural difficulties. So we must see and understand the impact of complex systemic pressures whilst resisting either becoming immersed in the difficulty of the person's experi-ence or *'prescribing'* services in a way that reassures the worker rather than actually helping the person (Moore, 2021). We must hear and respond to stories of personal challenge whilst listening keenly for the coping strat-egies that help the person get through. Where Strengths is oversimplified, this can mean glossing over or disregarding uncomfortable truths and a dismissive response to the painful realities of life.

Conflation with broader community Strengths-based models

It doesn't help that Strengths-based social work is often confused with community strengths-based models such as 'Asset Based Community Development' (ABCD). The aims and values of both individual and community-based models are similar as both support connected and empowered citizens. But whereas ABCD uses tools such as *'asset maps'* of the local area to develop community potential, Strengths-based social work uses narrative-based conversations to emphasise potential at the individual level. It may be a confused attempt to translate the asset mapping of ABCD into individual conversations that has led to the uncomfortably simplistic opening gambit of *'What are your strengths?'*. To be clear, a Strengths-based conversation is *not* a series of questions about what someone is good at; it's a conversation about whatever is important to the person at the time. The Strengths-based element is the social worker listening carefully for hints of strengths and resiliencies that have helped the person up until now and that might be built upon to help further in the future.

Relationships are key

The reality is that time-pressed assessments can focus on need and eligibility at the cost of understanding what really matters to the person. For real understanding of what's important, there must be genuine connection between the person and their social worker, and this is unlikely to arise from cursory question and answer sessions. Such understanding underpins the collaboration of a Strengths conversation. We've all seen tasks completed and processes followed without any real sense of the person; this is how relational practice can become buried under the forces of transactional process. Yet collaboration is difficult; genuine connection demands vulnerability from all involved. We give a little of ourselves when we connect to another and we open ourselves to the hurts they face. We tend to think our professional lives should somehow be separate from our own emotional experiences, so although we expect people to be open with us, we try to shut down our own defences. But it's exactly this emotional disconnect that can lead to process-driven practice-by-numbers. The collaboration of the Strengths approach demands two-way transformative connection.

Consider this story from practice:

As well as constant pain from a series of auto-immune related illnesses, Abi experienced frequent bouts of overwhelming depression. Meera, her new social worker, was at a loss to see how she might help. Abi's previous social worker had used a direct payment to set up gym membership. But Abi hadn't asked for this and never felt physically well enough to go. The fact that she was wasting public money made her feel even worse about herself.

Instead of talking about problems and possible sources of help and support (problem/solution), Meera asked Abi about her life and what was most important to her. Abi's priority was being as active and hands-on with her teenage children as her illness would allow. She mentioned that one way she managed this was by offering lifts in the car whenever she was well enough to drive. She thought this was probably as good a way as any to connect with teenagers. Before becoming unwell, Abi used to go to gigs and would take the children to festivals. Music had always been an important part of her life and although the car stereo was now broken, singing along in the car was a fun family tradition.

Meera felt sad for all that Abi's illness had cost the family but she also felt admiration for Abi's determination and approach to parenting. As she got into her own car and drove away, she noticed she'd automatically switched on her radio to lift her spirits and reflected on the importance of music for Abi and her children.

Following a further conversation, Meera and Abi decided to use a small direct payment to get Abi's car radio fixed. This didn't cure Abi's illness, lift her depression or make parenting teenagers any less tricky. But it did resolve one issue that made life a bit easier for Abi by capitalising on the resilience that her love of music created in its ability to sometimes distract and lift her mood. Music in the car made it more possible in a small but important way for Abi to do what matters most: to be a hands-on mum.

Without such attention to and use of the relationship created between them, Meera might have overlooked the admiration she felt for Abi and she might have missed the emotional connection that led to the love of music as a resilience upon which to build.

At what cost relationships?

Social work is relational but authentic connection creates vulnerability and can cause us to enact unconscious defence mechanisms designed to protect us from the difficult emotions of our work. Such defences serve an important protective function but they can also create unhelpful barriers to the clear thought required for helpful practice. So Abi's previous social worker unconsciously protected herself from the pain of Abi's situation by taking action and setting up gym membership. This reassured her that she'd done what she could but it didn't actually help Abi; it made her feel worse. Staying with the painful truth that Abi's situation will remain so difficult is an emotional challenge for Meera, but it has allowed her to connect with the reality of Abi's world and to recognise the presence and value of Abi's sources of resilience. So the resilience created by Abi's love of music and the importance of her car stereo is understood and the creative offer of support in the form of a working car radio can be arranged. This doesn't cure Abi's illness and resolve all the problems, but it does make it a bit easier for her to cope. The authentic connection and collaboration required of a Strengths approach to social work demands that we stay in the reality, see clearly and connect to what matters.

Contributions and need

There's more to Strengths approach than its catchy label would suggest. Abi's strengths as a loving and insightful mum, her love of music and her car might be the strengths headlines in her story, but she clearly has practical, medical and emotional needs caused by her illness as well as a driving need to contribute meaningfully by being present and useful to her children. We need to give as well as receive love, friendship and support. This symbiotic drive has been termed the *'reciprocity imperative'* (Richardson, 2020, p 180) and highlights the importance of contribution. Abi's role as Mum is an example of important personal contribution but contribution can also be about wider community responsibilities such as recycling or shopping locally. When we listen to stories and highlight strengths and resiliencies, it's also helpful to notice and highlight the many ways in which people are contributing to others. We all have needs, including a need to contribute. Social workers must talk about need and dependency without these becoming defining characteristics.

Relationships and Reciprocity

I propose a model of Relationships and Reciprocity (Moore, 2022) to build upon the affirming principles of Strengths approach while explicitly acknowledging need, dependency and the reciprocity imperative.

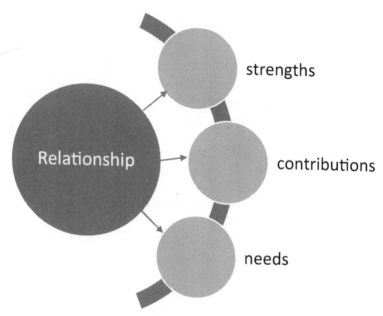

Figure 4.1 Model of Relationships and Reciprocity.

Such an approach recognises strengths, contributions and needs within the context of the authentic relationship that's necessary for genuine and helpful connection. Relationships and Reciprocity principles would build upon the existing principles of Strengths-based social work as they would include the following.

- A belief that focusing on deficiencies alone is not useful, so interest is in Strengths resiliencies, coping mechanisms and contributions while experiences of dependency are also attended to.

- Optimism; everyone has the capacity to contribute, reciprocate, learn and grow. Relationships are the container within which this can be communicated, encouraged and experienced.

- The relationship between person and social worker is key and is a source of discovery, understanding and containment.

- The person is the director of the helping process but there needs to be a trusting relationship in place in order to understand and authentically respond to their direction.

- Community is a source of potential support and an opportunity for reciprocity and contribution but meaningful connection with the person is needed for personalised understanding of what this means.

Relationships and Reciprocity emphasises the role of the relationship as the container for social work practice. It's based upon connections between people, so can't be transactionalised and made into a procedure. It demands the space, regard and care of thoughtful connection with recognition of the vulnerability this brings.

Conclusion

Strengths-based social work is not superficial; it's a difficult and emotionally demanding way of working that requires practice, reflection and resilience and offers a respectful and positive starting position for engagement.

But authentic relational connections expose us to a vulnerability that can be difficult to bear within the volume and pace of local authority social work. The Relationships and Reciprocity model offers the value base and affirmative approach of strengths and contributions while facing up to the reality of need and demanding the reflective space necessary for meaningful relationship-based practice. A reflective approach to relational practice opens us up to real connection with and appreciation of the people we meet. Such relationship-focused practice allows all participants to experience authentic connection and form the understanding and appreciation from which both trust and creativity can emerge.

References

BASW (2018) Professional Capabilities Framework. [online] Available at: www.basw.co.uk/pcf (accessed 2 November 2022).

Department of Health and Social Care (2014) *The Care Act*. [online] Available at: www.legislation.gov.uk/ukpga/2014/23/contents/enacted (accessed 14 November 2022).

Department of Health and Social Care (2018) Chief Social Worker for Adults Annual Report 2017–18. From Strength to Strength: Strengths-based Practice and Achieving Better Lives. [online] Available at: www.gov.uk/gov ernment/publications/chief-social-worker-for-adults-annual-report-2017-to-2018 (accessed 14 November 2022).

Department of Health and Social Care (2019) *Strengths-based Approach: Practice Framework and Practice Handbook*. [online] Available at: https://assets.publishing.service.gov.uk/government/uploads/system/uploads/attachment_data/file/778134/stengths-based-approach-practice-framework-and-handbook.pdf (accessed 14 November 2022).

Moore, T (2021) Strengths Approach Means Never Having to Ask Someone What They're Good At. *Social Work Cats and Rocket Science*. [online] Available at: https://socialworkcatsandrocketscience.com/2021/09/11/streng ths-approach-means-never-having-to-ask-someone-what-theyre-good-at (accessed 2 November 2022).

Moore, T (2022) Relationships and Reciprocity: Where Next for Strengths-based Social Work in Adult Social Care. *Journal of Social Work Practice*, 36(4): 451–63.

Nelson-Becker, H, Lloyd, L, Milne, A, Perry, E, Ray, M, Richards, S, Sullivan, M P, Tanner, D and Willis, P (2020) Strengths-based Social Work with Older People: A UK Perspective. In Mendenhall, A N and Carney, M M (eds) *Rooted in Strengths: Celebrating the Strengths Perspective in Social Work* (pp 327–46). University of Kansas Libraries.

Richardson, A J (2020) It's Personal: Lived Experiences of Adult Social Care and Social Work Practice in a Policy Context of Personalisation. PhD thesis at Tavistock and Portman NHS Foundation Trust/University of East Anglia.

Saleebey, D (1996) The Strengths Perspective in Social Work Practice. *Social Work*, 41(3): 296–305.

Social Work England (2019) Professional Standards. [online] Available at: www.socialworkengland.org.uk/standards/professional-standards (accessed 2 November 2022).

Weick, A, Rapp, C, Sullivan, W P and Kisthardt, W (1989) A Strengths Perspective for Social Work Practice. *Social Work*, 34(4): 350–4.

CHAPTER 5

SAFEGUARDING ADULTS

Fran Leddra

Introduction

I have to confess it has taken me a while to write this opening paragraph. For much of my 35-year career I have worked in safeguarding and I believe good safeguarding practice makes a difference to people's lives. Indeed, I believe that at times it can be life-saving. I also advocate good clear processes, policies, guidance and governance. At the heart of good safeguarding is a type of order that should tell a personal story from beginning to end, showing critical thinking and theory so the decisions and actions taken lead to increased safety. Even if risk remains.

So why has it been difficult to set the scene of this chapter? It's because I'm going to contradict some of that and challenge the concept that all those processes, policies and practices keep people safe. They help. Yes, they provide a clear framework across partnerships to respond to abuse and, to some degree, help prevent abuse occurring. But do they help keep people safe? How can they? As we sit in our offices or even when out and about in our communities, we can only ever support people, we can't live someone's life and be with them 24/7. Nor can we personally, or even collectively within our partnerships, keep people safe. And yet everywhere in adult safeguarding, we see the statement that the work we do protects people from harm. We need to accept that the feeling of safety will always be intensely personal, as will the sense of harm. The extent to which we can protect people from harm will be dependent on that person's life experiences, their relationships and the degree to which they see risk as inherent to life.

Risk and safeguarding

This leads me to my next thought. Risk management plans do not prevent risk. They are a case management tool that we can use to show our considerations of a person's situation, provide an audit trail of our thinking. But they will rarely become a meaningful document for the person. I've always advocated good risk management plans; they can be a really good tool to set down critical thinking and identify gaps that lead us to explore further. But most people will continue to live their lives without the risk management plan prominent in their thinking. In all my years of practice I've never heard anyone say they checked their risk management plan before taking a risk! Risk management plans help professionals demonstrate the steps they take to manage risk. But let's not pretend they remove risk.

We often confuse risk with safeguarding, and can be so procedural and over-bureaucratic in our practice that we may not always support people in a meaningful way. Most organisations, but especially local authorities, spend a lot of time and resources on adult safeguarding, but may still have a disconnect with their local communities. That's not to underplay the work safeguarding boards do in raising awareness, engaging with people with lived experience and promoting partnership working so that we can provide the best response to safeguarding situations. I simply want to acknowledge that the professional world of adult safeguarding is likely to be far removed from most citizens' experiences.

Jargon

That includes the language we use. There's so much jargon, and if we want to genuinely connect and communicate we must consider how we use language. This is hardly a new discussion point; we've been debating language in social work for years. I wrote a student assignment on this very subject it in 1994! Yet we still don't always get it right. The term 'safeguarding' itself will be jargon for most people and describing someone as 'vulnerable' can mean many different things. When I had the privilege of meeting many people with lived experience in my role as Chief Social Worker, the use of terminology frequently came up. This was particularly so during the Covid pandemic where the term 'most vulnerable in society' was used in daily in the media and by politicians. Overwhelmingly, people didn't like it; at best it's patronising and at worst quite insulting.

No group of people is 'inherently vulnerable'. If a group is experiencing vulnerability in a particular situation, setting, system or society, then that vulnerability is being produced by other people and circumstances. When we refer to 'vulnerable groups', the implication is that the vulnerability is 'built-in'; that it's a deficit, a condition internal to that group. This implies our role as professionals is to 'save' people from their vulnerability. This is why we're often criticised for the term being patronising. If we want to practise safeguarding in a truly inclusive way and a way in which we promote co-production, then we need to ditch this generic term.

Let's face it, all of us at some times in our life will be vulnerable to something, referring to the people we support as 'the vulnerable' is simply not acceptable. It sets us apart, creates a 'them and us', and further distances us from the people and communities we want to engage with and support in relation to safeguarding.

We have a fair amount to consider and not always the space and time to do so. This chapter uses stories to explore that tension and illustrate the importance of the relationships we build with people, neighbourhoods and communities. It looks at when we need to intervene, when we need to take a step back and when we need to do something different.

Meeting a Camerado

I had the pleasure of meeting up with Maff Potts recently over a tasty roasted vegetable sharing platter (we have photos to prove it!). The restaurant itself is a social enterprise supporting people who need to get back on their feet, learn new skills and get out to work. Maff is founder of Camerados. It's not an organisation, and he's very quick to point that out.

He definitely doesn't want to try and '*fix*' people. He describes Camerados as a '*Movement that's about people looking out for one another*'. It's based on people being able to '*just be themselves in a space that's warm and inviting and to also be a bit silly*'. It doesn't reach out to anyone specific, it simply creates public living room spaces and people come. The outcome is whatever people get out of the space at the time. It encourages an organic growth of human relationships. Some will be fleeting, others may last a while, but it recognises that people don't always want a service, or to see a professional; they may just want another person in their neighbourhood to talk to, or a space to have a comfy seat, play some music and have a think. Wherever public living rooms pop up, they are warmly received. They are human spaces.

Camerados has six main principles.

1. It's ok to be a bit rubbish.

2. Don't fix one another, we are just alongside.

3. Have fun, to be silly is to be human.

4. Mix with people who are not like you.

5. We can disagree respectively.

6. If someone is struggling, ask them to help you.

Sounds fluffy but it's not; their website suggests it can save lives (Camerados, nd). For me, this is safeguarding, but not in a way we know it. It's leaving people to simply '*be*' within their communities. Those moments when people may, for a while, not feel so lonely or isolated and might find support in another. Maybe someone will say something that makes a difference or leads someone to reach out for support – or maybe not.

It resonates with what we do in adult social care, as the opening of the Care Act says:

> the core purpose of adult care and support is to help people achieve the outcomes that matter to them in their life.

Yet here comes the dilemma. Maff tells me that, having created the spaces, professional organisations are saying *'what about safeguarding?'* *'Should some notice or something go up in the public living rooms?'* *'Do they have a policy?'* *'Really?'*, I say, knowing actually that of course they would say that; public living rooms pop up in various local authority areas and local authorities are concerned with safeguarding. So we talk it through. What's the issue? What difference would it make? Would it actually put people off confiding in someone and cause more risk? Isn't it the case that raising safeguarding awareness is a good thing? Aren't posters often put up in shops and cafes – so what's the big deal?

Balancing the tension between the need for people to feel safe and for people to feel free to get on with their own lives is complex, and as a profession and a society we need to think this through. But my hunch is that any stifling of the organic nature of Camerados will not be a good thing.

I'm leaving this as a discussion point: we should debate in practice. What are we there for? When do we step back and allow people to just be? When do we impose some boundaries and when do we take action?

Safeguarding adults shouldn't start with statutory authorities putting in a process. We all have a basic human right to be safe and free from abuse. It should start with all of us trusting friends, neighbours, communities and building relationships in a safe environment where we can talk and maybe tell our story. Maybe that will lead to someone seeking more professional support, maybe it won't. There will always be people wanting to exploit or harm others. Safeguarding practice doesn't stop that. What difference can policy make? Is its real purpose to protect the organisation rather than the individual?

The neighbour and the football team

I remember working alongside a particularly gifted social worker. She naturally understood the importance of relationships and found innovative ways of encouraging strong connections with the people with whom she worked that included their neighbours and their communities. Her commitment to relationships wasn't just about her relationship with the individual;

she recognised this could sometimes be superficial, short term and not what would sustain a person in the long run. Her commitment was to the families and neighbours around them; so that when she needed to step back she had already facilitated real connections and friendships.

She was particularly challenged by a young autistic man who was being criminally exploited. He didn't particularly relate to her as a 40-something woman, but that didn't stop her tirelessly walking alongside him, helping him to form more positive relationships with his mother, his siblings and his neighbours and to cut his ties with the criminal gangs that were exploiting him. He really wanted a change of life, but the pull of his peers was much stronger than the traditional services such as the talking therapies which were on offer but which he never attended. Safeguarding plans were in place, but he wasn't interested and continued to miss appointments with the professionals from whom he felt totally disconnected. He was a young man moving into adulthood and requiring a flexible safeguarding response.

His social worker wasn't going to give up and kept regular appointments with him at his home, whether he turned up or not. His mother was at a loss about what to do to support her son and the arguments in the house were causing neighbour conflict on top of everything else. One of the most important steps the social worker took was (with the family's permission) to knock on the neighbour's door and explain what had been going on. The social worker gently mediated between the two families so they could rebuild their previously warm relationship. This led to them creating their own plan, so when the young man's mother needed support the neighbour would help, or even call the social worker if they needed her.

Knowing this young man liked football, the social worker also reached out to the local football team. With his permission, she told his story and they offered him some time at the club. Contact with positive male role models helped him gradually break away from his disruptive peers. He even handed over his phone as it was being used to pull him back into criminal activity. The social worker would occasionally pop in to see him at the football club where she could see he was becoming far more communicative and independent.

Within the year, with the help of the neighbour, the football team and the social worker, the young man had broken away from the criminal gangs and returned to college.

This was a real success story. With his mother and neighbour's help, the young man even reconnected with his church. We wanted to know what made the difference for him and he told us he felt safer when his neighbour knew what was going on as this helped his relationship with his mum. He preferred to talk to the men in the football club than to his social worker or therapists, but he respected what his social worker had done for him. His social worker felt she had to involve members of his community because traditional methods of support had made no difference and the young man had been completely disengaged with statutory services. But she could see his potential and, while there were risks to her approach, the risks to which he was already exposed were much greater.

What strikes me about this story is its simplicity. Instead of offering a statutory, service-led response to a safeguarding situation, the social worker looked to what was on offer in the community.

This particular social worker has many stories like this to tell because she's willing to work with risk and practice in a truly strength-based way. Her manager and her team support her in this showing how leadership matters in creating the right environment for practitioners to do things differently.

The carpenter

This next story illustrates community-based safeguarding. It started with a referral that an elderly gentleman was sleeping in a shop doorway, drunk and very unwell. Everyone in the neighbourhood knew him to the extent that he had almost become invisible, but this day he was blocking a shop doorway and they wanted him moved. The man was taken to hospital where the social worker visited him. There had been several safeguarding plans over the years but none had made a difference, and he continued to be addicted to alcohol. He wasn't homeless but was always at risk of losing his tenancy because of his inability to control his drinking. Rather than just repeat what everyone had done in the past, the social worker tried a different approach to working with him and called upon the Local Area Co-ordinator to become involved. The Local Area Co-ordinator's role is firmly embedded within the neighbourhood. She introduced the man to various neighbourhood groups, including a men's group. Here, other group members asked him about his life instead of his addiction. They discovered he'd been a carpenter. This led to him being linked to a place where people volunteered their skills to help others who needed practical support. There were many people in need of a carpenter.

Again, it sounds simple, but we all know it's not. There's skill in helping people in a way that enables relationships to come first and process second. This work doesn't need to be costly, and through many years' experience I've come to the belief that when we do the right thing, it's often the most cost-effective thing to do too.

It's the genuine friendships that help us develop a sense of belonging and safety. Good safeguarding practice should look beyond the planning and the professional input to how we can support more meaningful relationships.

Final thoughts

I know there are many inspirational stories across the country and these are not unique, but I also think they are not common enough. We talk about 'strengths-based community-led' support, but rarely see it embedded into organisational culture and we shy away from it when it comes to safeguarding. We can be elitist, thinking we know best and that safeguarding is the highest risk element of our service, requiring specialist skills. That may be partially true, but the greatest skill of all is helping people build relationships and knowing when to step back.

You might read this and think about the worst-case scenario where this approach wouldn't work. For those of us who advocate a different way of working, we are used to these challenges, and see many of them as valid. Our general approach, however, should not be to design safeguarding services only to meet the worst-case scenarios. Safeguarding is more nuanced and requires debate and discussion about doing thing differently. The best practice entails a proactive reach-out to people's communities. It's here that people are more likely to find the help they need to keep themselves safe.

Reflections

- Considering the points made in relation to community-based groups such as Camerados, what do you think the role of safeguarding should be?
- What do think may prevent social workers from taking a more community-based approach to safeguarding? How might you approach this?
- What are the advantages and the risks in taking this approach?

Reference

Camerados (nd) Camerados. [online] Available at: www.camerados.org (accessed 24 October 2022).

CHAPTER 6

A REFLECTION ON ONLINE RELATIONSHIPS AND THE CHANGING LANDSCAPE OF PRACTICE

Claudia Megele

Introduction

Over a decade ago I wrote an article, 'Social Care in the E-Professionalism Era' (Megele, 2012), which reflected on some of the challenges and implications of social media for social work practice. There were strong reactions to that article, ranging from a social care practitioner who shared his own positive experience of using social media in practice to an anonymous account who commented:

> ... so thank you for writing this patronising rubbish. If a qualified and registered social worker doesn't know how to conduct themselves at all times ... they do not deserve to be a social worker.

> Of course I am talking as an anachronism who doesn't indulge in online relationships ... e-mail is great ... just like writing a letter ... but facebook and its like are for foolish and immature narcissists who are contributing to a new social cancer.

A lot has changed since then as the profession has gained appreciation of the complexity of online relationships and ethics. The Covid-19 pandemic further accelerated the use and application of digital technologies across a vast array of services and professions ranging from online shopping to GP consultations. And social workers have adopted creative ways of engaging and working with people online from social work home visits to child protection conferences.

Today, social media and digital technologies are an integral part of children and young people's identity, relationships and development. They're an integral part of empowering most adults who access services. This chapter will consider online relationships and some of the differences from offline relationships. It must, however, be emphasised that most young people see their relationships and interactions as a continuous experience rather than online versus offline.

A word on digital professionalism or e-professionalism

The changing relationship between humans and technology underscores the need for digital professionalism or e-professionalism. So, what is digital professionalism?

The principles of digital professionalism are similar to those of traditional face-to-face professionalism, but they require professionals to extend and apply the profession's ethics and values in a meaningful and effective manner within a digital context. However, to think that digital professionalism is simply an extension of traditional face-to-face professionalism would be to miss the complexity of online relationships. Digital professionalism also includes the ability to identify and effectively manage new risks and opportunities and to be able to use digital and social technologies effectively to complement and enhance practice and its outcomes.

Digital professionalism can be thought of as the intersection of face-to-face professional ethics, values and principles vis-à-vis the roles, opportunities, risks and challenges of digital and social media technologies. All this within the context of the shifting social, cultural and political landscape in which professionals operate. It's within this intersection that digital professionalism can be achieved (see Figure 6.1) (Megele, 2018).

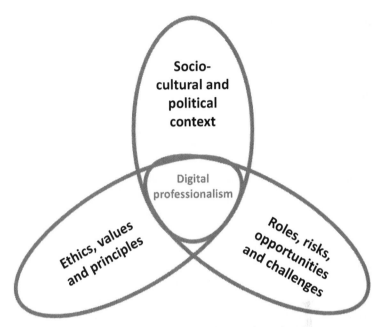

Figure 6.1 Digital professionalism and overlapping boundaries.

A changing practice landscape

Although social work values don't change significantly online versus offline, there are significant differences between online and offline behaviours and environment that require specific knowledge, skills and capabilities to practice effectively while maintaining appropriate professional boundaries online. There is huge potential in social media and digital technologies. Below are some examples of positive application in practice as well as new forms of online risks and harm.

Positive online practice

Social media and digital technologies present unlimited possibilities for creativity and positive affirmation of identity, relationships and experience. For example, by offering online child protection conferences and review meetings, more young people have been able to participate and some young people have had the opportunity to chair their own review meetings. This has helped boost young people's confidence and identity and allowed for them to be better heard and more effectively inform the actions and decisions of parents and professionals.

Another example of good digital practice is merging story-telling with care for people with dementia. This enables sharing of learning about challenges faced through the everyday stories of people who experience them. Digital life story books can be used to support and enhance the individual identity. Similar to traditional life story books, digital versions follow a chrono-logical order and can be divided into various segments such as: childhood, adolescence/teenage life, mid-life, career and so on until the present. They can include photographic and other materials such as images of significant others, favourite places, activities, songs, music, movie clips and recording of events. These can be accompanied by narration and quotations from part-ners, loved ones and so on. Such story books help rekindle memories and evoke emotions associated with significant moments in the person's life and can enrich the person's present-day experience.

New forms and dimensions of risk and harm

From everyday misunderstandings or exposure to age-inappropriate or developmentally inappropriate content to aggression, bullying, stalking, grooming, sexual abuse, radicalisation and other forms of online harm and abuse, social media platforms present a range of challenges and risks. Below is an example of one such new risk presented in a landmark case that for the first time recognised digital assault as a criminal offence.

Digital assault

In December 2016, when Kurt Eichenwald opened a tweet from an anonymous twitter user, the message 'YOU DESERVE A SEIZURE FOR YOUR POSTS' appeared in capital letters along with a blinding strobe light. Eichenwald immediately suffered a serious seizure. This was reported to the FBI and subsequent investigations identified 29-year-old John Rayne Rivello, an army veteran, as the person responsible for the tweet. After pursuing a search warrant, investigators found Twitter direct messages in which Rivello had discussed Eichenwald, said he hoped his message would send him into a seizure and said he was waiting to see if the writer died. Investigators also searched Rivello's digital accounts and found a screenshot of Eichenwald's Wikipedia page that had been altered to show a fake date of death on 16 December 2016, the day after the strobe light attack. This account also contained screenshots of www.epilepsy.com with a list of commonly reported epilepsy seizure triggers.

Eichenwald is an American journalist and had written several articles about Trump, his campaign and his own conflict of interest in the 2016 US presidential election. Rivello, a staunch Trump follower, had discovered that Eichenwald experienced epilepsy, was photosensitive and that the strobe of light could result in seizure. In March 2017, about three months after Eichenwald's seizure, the FBI arrested and charged Rivello with criminal cyberstalking with the intent to kill or cause bodily harm.

There have been many online attacks with physical consequences such as attacks on electrical grids or air traffic control systems and others. However, this was a targeted attack that was personal, using a simple tweet. There have been many lawsuits involving stalking and cyberbullying, but these cases focused on how online content, such as abusive, aggressive or disparaging messages and pictures can harm victims emotionally and even result in increased risk of suicide. In this case, however, there was evidence to suggest that Rivello had designed the attack based on Eichenwald's medical condition with the intent to cause bodily harm. In court, Eichenwald's lawyer argued: *'This electronic message was no different than a bomb sent in the mail or anthrax sent in an envelope ... It triggers a physical effect.'*

This is a landmark case. For the first time, the court found the defendant to be guilty of digital assault. Since this case, there have been several other instances of strobe attacks online, and in 2018 the Twitter account of the Epilepsy Foundation in America was subject a to a similar mass attack on all its followers.

These are examples of the new forms of harm and there are many others that demonstrate how social media and digital technologies can result in new risk or change the impact and implications of risks.

There are a number of factors that influence and present new challenges for relationships. Below is a description of some of the more important factors that influence online relationships.

Online disinhibition effect

In face-to-face interactions, we don't always say what we think or feel; we often exercise restraint and express ourselves in ways we consider appropriate for a given conversation or situation. Consciously or unconsciously, most people can think about their online identities and interactions as separate from their offline identity and sense of who they are. This separation of self from our online postings can generate a sense of disinhibition and can be helpful if we critically consider what we're posting and what it says about our identity and sense of self. Such benign disinhibition can also be helpful in expressing our thoughts, feelings and opinions. However, the splitting of online and offline identity can also generate a level of disinhibition that can be unhelpful and result in online aggression or behaviours such as bullying, stalking, grooming and so on.

The online disinhibition effect was first discussed by John Suler (2004) and can operate in two directions. The disinhibition effect can result in the disclosure of personal emotions and information by the individual. It may also result in more expansive behaviour, such as unusual acts of kindness or generosity. These behaviours are referred to as *'benign disinhibition'* (Suler, 2004, p 321). However, online disinhibition can also result in conflict, threats, production or use of pornography, sexting, harassment or other aggressive behaviours. This is referred to as *'toxic disinhibition'*. Online disinhibition has an important impact on online relationships and can be a double-edged sword where, on the one hand, people form quicker friendships and relationships while, on the other hand, relationships can fall apart more quickly.

Dissociative anonymity

Although it's difficult to achieve a high degree of anonymity, people can hide or alter their identity and present different or multiple identities online. People can also create online identities with no name or a false name. This can lead to a sense of anonymity, and *online anonymity* refers to one's perception of being unidentifiable online.

Through use of online persona and profiles, personal pages, avatars and usernames (including fictitious or pseudo names) as well as creation of online profiles, one can create and project a self and way of being that is either similar or quite different from one's offline persona in terms of age, background, personality, physical appearance and even gender, lifestyle and lived experiences.

Anonymity offers positive opportunities as well as challenges. For example, anonymity allows young people to create and experiment with different online identities and, depending on how this is used and managed, can have a positive or negative impact for their development. The concept of anonymity is relative and more perception than reality, but it can still weaken the link between the individual and their behaviour, creating a sense of dissociation from online behaviour and avoidance of any eventual negative consequences while reaping its rewards. This in turn can reinforce the online disinhibition effect and result in aggression, transgressions, abuse, fraud, crime and other offensive and harmful behaviours.

Invisibility

In many text-based online environments, people can't see each other. For example, when people participate in forums, read/comment on a blog or website, tweet, retweet, *'like'* or make online postings, they can't see others in-person and might not even know if anyone else is present in that online space.

This offers the opportunity to try new ideas and behave in ways that are different from their offline behaviour. Although both invisibility and dissociative anonymity help people hide their identity, they're not the same thing although they compound each other's effect. For example, people in an online forum may know a lot about each other but they still can't see or hear each other and this increases the disinhibition effect (Suler, 2004; Megele, 2014; Megele and Buzzi, 2017). Depending on how it's used, the combination of anonymity and invisibility can have a positive and empowering effect, such as empowering whistleblowers to speak truth to power, or a negative and disempowering effect when it is used for aggression, transgression or abuse.

Asynchronicity

While in-person, face-to-face interactions occur in real-time and require immediate response, most online interactions are asynchronous; they are a sequence of online postings and it's acceptable that one may not receive an immediate response from the person with whom one is communicating (this may be due to a range of factors such as the other person being busy with something else and responding when they find the time to return to the conversation). For example, emails, online comments or other similar postings may take minutes, hours, days or even months before receiving a reply (Megele and Buzzi, 2017). Not having to respond immediately reduces the cognitive demand for the individual and offers them the opportunity to think about and formulate their response and frame their answer.

Minimisation of status and authority

Cyberspace has a levelling effect in the sense that one's status, authority or power offline seems to be of little impact online and this creates a sort of 'equality' as users tend to start interactions as equals (Suler, 2004). Offline, authority figures' power and status are expressed and observed through social symbols such as dress, possessions and body language, most of which are absent or expressed differently in online environments. Indeed, even if people are aware of the offline power and status of a given individual, their authority is less visible and hence has less influence on their persona and interactions online than offline.

In face-to-face interactions people are aware of others' presence and authority and fear of embarrassment, disapproval or punishment moderates and regulates their interactions. But, online, the environment feels more like a peer relationship and this generates a diminished sense/perception of others' authority. Even interactions with authorities are more disinhibited as people are more willing to speak out and misbehave (Suler, 2004; Buzzi and Megele, 2022).

The combination of the above factors combined with ease of online connection and communication generates a sense of closeness and familiarity that can influence one's perception of relationships and boundaries, and this can have important implications for practice. So it's important that social workers are more explicit and intentional in their online postings, connections and communications.

Identity prism

Identity prism (Figure 6.2) offers social workers a practical tool to think about and evaluate their online postings, identities and relationships.

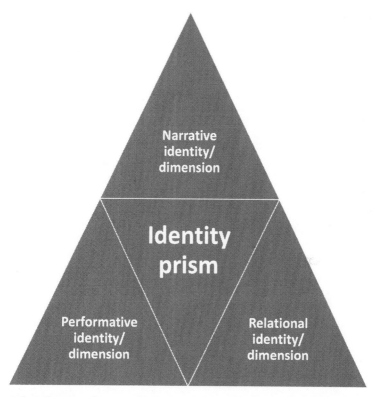

Thinking about online identities and postings

Figure 6.2 Identity prism.

Each online identity and posting can be thought of as three interlinked and complementing aspects that reflect the different ways they may be constructed, looked at and perceived.

Narrative aspect

Online postings and activities are a form of self-expression and tell a story about people's identity and self-narrative. Being clear and intentional about our online activities requires us to ask ourselves what each online posting says about our identity and self-narrative and how each affects our online persona and sense of who we are. *'Is this authentic and is this what I want to present about myself?' 'What are its implications for my practice and professional identity?'*

Performance aspect

Online postings and activities can be considered as performance before an online audience. A helpful question to ask of ourselves might be: *'how is my online activity, behaviour and performance perceived or understood by my audience and others?'* The audience may be intended or unintended and may result in intended or unintended meaning. Reflection on this meaning can improve our understanding of context and our online relationships.

Relational aspect

Online postings and activities can also be considered in the context of relationships or interactions with others. Helpful questions to ask ourselves might be: *'what do my online postings and activities say about my relationships and how do they position me in relation to others?' 'How does this influence my own and others' perception of boundaries and their relationship with me and what are the implications of this for co-production and working with people who access services?'* and *'What are the implications of this for my professional identity and professional relationships?'*

The Identity Prism tool offers a lens to reflect upon the multidimensional implications of online postings and activities. It helps us consider how online activity relates to our professional identity. This helps social workers develop their online identity in positive ways as well as to think about online identities and activities of people who access services.

A changing landscape: The commodifying of values, identities and relationships

A 22-year-old TikTok influencer walks up to an older woman sitting in a mall, drinking her takeaway coffee. He gives her a bouquet of flowers, saying: *'Sorry to bother you, is it OK if you can just hold these?'* Then he puts his backpack on the ground and pulls out a parka before walking off, saying, *'have a lovely day'* and leaving the woman with flowers. The woman notices that another young man had been filming the interaction and asks: *'Did you film that?'* and the young man replies *'No, no'*.

In another video, the influencer distracts a grocery shopper by pretending she has dropped money on the floor. As she turns away to search for it, the influencer places money in one of her shopping bags. Then he says *'Oh, have a good day'*, and walks away as the woman returns to the checkout desk. She is then told by the cashier that the man had paid for her groceries. In the video the woman appears to have a muted reaction, smiling faintly, and later appears to be pointing in the direction of the young man with an upset look on her face.

These videos were posted on TikTok as random acts of kindness by the influencer for his three million followers and have received more than 59 million views. It must be said that this influencer makes between $10,000 to $15,000 a month from such videos through brand partnerships and sponsored posts. However, when an Australian paper approached the older woman in the first video, asking her what she thought about receiving the flowers, she stated that she felt *'dehumanised'*.

The influencer in question has received positive feedback from some viewers who praised his videos, with one person saying: *'I swear you are the best'*, and another stating: *'You're so filled with kindness. Love it.'* However, other viewers have criticised his behaviour, raising the issue of lack of consent, claiming he is exploiting strangers and calling him *'exploitation king'*. One viewer commented: *'If you record yourself doing a selfless deed, is it still really ALL that selfless???'* and another stated: *'Monetising your exploitation of strangers and in exchange they get a bag of fast food ...'*.

In an increasingly digital society with diminishing privacy, such events high-light the importance of consent and also the question raised by the viewer about whether it's still a *'selfless'* act of kindness when you video such events and make significant amounts of money. What are the implications of such behaviours and cultures for people's dignity, identity and self-narrative? This is an important question from a societal as well as practice perspective. Immersed in a culture of voyeurism with increasing infringement of individual privacy, social workers like others may have the urge to share their experience or an *'act of kindness'*. But before sharing one's own experience, it's important to reflect on the implications of such sharing for one's own as well as others' dignity and identity. We need to consider whether such sharing or actions are empowering for the practitioner and the people we work with or whether they might undermine anyone's position or image in some ways. What one may portray as an *'act of kindness'* may actually reflect social stereotypes and embed judgement about people's identities. Worse, it may be intentional commodification and exploitation of values, identities and relationships. I can't judge the intentions of the influencer described above but the denial of the young man filming the event when asked *'Did you film that?'* and the sub-sequent posting of the video on TikTok raise ethical questions about consent and instrumentalisation of people for financial gain.

Such behaviours, attitudes and cultures can present a challenge in practice as they are given visibility and increasingly normalised and emulated by other adults and young people.

Changing intimacy and relationships

From online friending to online dating, sites present new ways of developing and maintaining relationships. On the one hand, this allows for a larger and more diverse social network where one's friendships can span across cultures and geographic boundaries. There is evidence that online dating sites have resulted in increased intercultural relationships among couples which can contribute to a more diverse and equal society. On the other hand, online dating sites have also been used for fraud, abuse and exploitation.

The increasing influence of social media and digital technologies in relationships has also led to new expressions and expectations of intimacy that can result in safeguarding challenges. For example, sharing of personal nude pictures in the context of couple relationships has become a new way of seeking and expressing intimacy, with some advocates arguing that this represents a safer alternative to physical intercourse. However, abuse of such images, often in cases of relationship breakdown, can be damaging to one or both parties and can result in significant safeguarding challenges.

The shifting boundaries of personal and professionalism and the need for authenticity

The above factors have a significant impact on online relationships as while, on the one hand, they can facilitate communication, personal expression and relationships, on the other hand, they can result in transgression, aggression and abuse.

The Covid-19 pandemic has demonstrated the enormous positive potential and value of social media and digital technologies to develop and maintain connections, communication and relationships. However, it has also highlighted the ease of misunderstanding and multiple other practical and ethical challenges of online relationships. The advent of online visits, working from home and other uses of online platforms has further blurred the boundaries of personal and professional spheres.

Traditionally the distinction between personal and professional roles were conceptualised as functions of physical space and location. The separation of workplace from home provided a clear distinction between public and private spheres with two distinct audiences and expected behaviours; professional identity and behaviour was confined to workplace with colleagues while private relationships and behaviour were contained within the private sphere of home with family and friends.

But this notion of identity bound by location and physical boundaries has been destabilised by increasing penetration of digital technologies in every sphere of life. The lack of physical boundaries online and increasing use of work from home has challenged the separation of audiences, expectations and behaviours. This increasing overlap between spheres of life and diversity of audiences requires consistency in one's behaviour, thoughts and self-presentations. This highlights the importance of authenticity of identities.

Conclusion

Relationships are multidimensional and complex, and while social media and digital technologies offer unlimited potential for connection, and enhancement of relationships and identities, they also have the potential to flatten relationships into the projection of a false image, devoid of meaning and authenticity onto a digital screen. The challenge in practice is the establishment of digital and e-professionalism that offers balanced appreciation of the opportunities and risks of online relationships and postings and their associated ethical and practical and professional implications.

Reflections

- What are some of your reflections about online relationships and the changing notion and expectations of relationships?

- What are some of your learnings from this chapter and which points did you find most relevant to your practice and why?

- How does your learning from this chapter influence your practice? What difference does it make and why?

References

Buzzi, P and Megele, C (2022) *Social Work, Tango and Magic: Making a Difference in Your Work with Children and Families*. London: Jessica Kingsley Publishers.

Megele, C (2012) Social Care in the E-Professionalism Era. *The Guardian*. [online] Available at: www.theguardian.com/social-care-network/2012/apr/25/eprofessionalism-social-care (accessed 8 November 2022).

Megele, C (2014) Theorizing Twitter Chat. *Journal of Perspectives in Applied Academic Practice*, 2(2). https://doi.org/10.14297/jpaap.v2i2.106.

Megele, C (2018) Social Media, Digital Professionalism and CPD: Strategic Briefing. Research in Practice. [online] Available at: www.researchinpractice. org.uk/children/publications/2018/december/social-media-digital-professionalism-and-cpd-strategic-briefing-2018/ (accessed 8 November 2022).

Megele, C and Buzzi, P (2017) *Safeguarding Adults Online*. Bristol: Policy Press.

Suler, J R (2004) The Online Disinhibition Effect. *CyberPsychology & Behavior*, 7(3): 321–6.

CHAPTER 7

HUMAN RIGHTS AND SOCIAL WORK

Hannah Scaife

Dedicated to Kage. You are absolutely wonderful.

Introduction

Clenton Farquharson, MBE, describes social care support as enabling him to

> *do what everyone else considers ordinary. Only when that becomes impossible do you realise the importance of these ordinary activities. They are precious. This ordinary stuff is the stuff of life.*

My chapter focuses on this *'ordinary stuff'*. It is integral to social work with adults but, ironically, it's also part of what makes it hard for us to describe the importance of our role because, to an outsider, it can look unexceptional. I will explore how this stuff is not only precious, *'the stuff of life'*, but also fundamental to what makes a person feel human, heard and respected.

Fundamentally, people share very similar and straightforward life goals. These have been summed up beautifully by Social Care Future as:

We all want to live in the place we call home, with the people and things we love, in communities where we look out for one another, doing things that matter to us.

(Social Care Future, 2022)

In her book *Radical Help*, Hilary Cottam says,

Our current welfare systems have a logic that runs like this: assess me, refer me, manage me. These systems count inputs (buildings and professional time) and outputs (reduced risk behaviours). They restrict access and try to manage costs.

(Cottam, 2018, p 197)

The constant push to transactional processes means people are categorised by eligibility criteria, diagnoses and risk. Services have clear remits for working that can't be crossed. Success criteria includes demand management or steering people away from services because services are too under-resourced to help. This disempowers people who can be expected to wait months to see a professional and might then be told they don't meet the criteria for that team's service.

Across social care, we're moving towards strengths-based and trauma-aware approaches. At the heart of this is understanding people as humans, with individual stories, hopes and dreams. One of the most awesome skills of social workers is our ability to listen. We build relationships with people who for very good reasons may find it hard to allow trust. Through these relationships, we help people feel they have the cushioning to try new things, take risks and dare to believe their version of a good life may be within their reach. So many times, I've heard people say their social worker made the difference because they '*believed in them when they were struggling to believe in themselves*'.

But there's a downside to these approaches. They can become too focused on a person's individual responsibility to change what isn't working in their lives. The idea of the '*big society*' that exists to support us all as long as we connect, feel motivated and help ourselves doesn't take account of the personal and structural disadvantages faced by many people. We know life isn't fair and equal and this is where a passion for human rights and social justice is essential for good social work practice.

Human rights

Social work and human rights are inextricably linked in the following ways.

- Human rights as a *legal framework* that provides structure, definitions of rights, duties and responsibilities and a template for action.
- Human rights as a *perspective* that informs our values and actions in practice (Spreadbury and Hubbard, 2020, p 21).

The rights that we commonly see breached in social work include the following.

- Article 2 of the Human Rights Act, 1998: right to life, which is an absolute right and also one which gives us (as agents of the state) an obligation in most cases to act to protect life.
- Article 3: freedom from torture and inhuman and degrading treatment, also an absolute right.
- Article 5: right to liberty and security of person, which is not absolute because there are circumstances where someone could be lawfully detained or deprived of their freedoms.
- Article 6: right to a fair trial or fair and public hearing – very important in the context of making decisions under the Mental Capacity Act, 2005 or Mental Health Act, 1983.
- Article 8: respect for private and family life, home and correspondence, also not an absolute right, but something we must always consider as we walk that delicate line between rights, risks and responsibilities.

Throughout this chapter, I will briefly reference when human rights are compromised, and you will see that this occurs in everyday situations and often goes unnoticed.

Journey into the *'messy stuff'*

My favourite description of social work is

> Social work is about life, treasuring humanity, building connections, sharing and promoting fairness. It is about creativity, care and love- being there to help people overcome obstacles and oppression that hold them back ... a social worker should be someone to trust and

believe in – someone who helps you believe in yourself. Sometimes we must hold boundaries, protect rights, advocate and challenge. We are always in the midst of the messy stuff, finding ways forwards.

(Allen, 2018, p 27)

I want to take you on a journey into the *'messy stuff'* of social work. I hope to make human rights and social justice come to life in the stories of everyday people encountering social workers as they move through difficult circumstances outside of their control. To explore when the ordinary becomes extraordinary due to discrimination and other barriers. In the spirit of *'nothing about us without us'* I've asked some people about their experiences and been given their permission to share their stories with you. These stories describe situations where human rights have been compromised and social workers have felt conflicted as they've navigated complex and contradictory legal powers and duties, working in contexts where the *'greater good'* is more of a focus than an individual's needs, wishes or feelings, or in systems or institutions where the process overrides the person. Names are, of course, all changed.

Theo

Theo's story was told to me by his mum, Anna. Theo was 17 years old and living at home with his mum (a general nurse), his dad (a mental health nurse) and his three siblings. Theo lives with severe autism and attended a specialist school. In January 2019, a CT head scan revealed that he had decay in three teeth and impacted wisdom teeth. Theo was referred to dentistry, but the referral was delayed. Theo doesn't have capacity to consent to dental treatment and can't be examined without a general anaesthetic, so he was referred again, this time to Special Dentistry. Finally, in August 2019, plans began to be formulated for Theo to attend his dental examination.

But in September 2019 he appeared to be struggling to cope with his pain. Anna described it as an *'awful, awful time'*. Theo wasn't sleeping and he was banging his head against walls. At school he banged his head so hard that he removed a whole reinforced glass window. He was covered in bruises and experiencing signs of concussion, but Anna couldn't get him seen by either his GP or his paediatrician. Theo was taken to A&E with visible bruising, possible concussion and skull fracture.

At a multidisciplinary meeting, it was decided that, due to his new head injury, Theo couldn't be managed in a dental hospital and the procedure needed to take place in a general hospital. Anna was desperate to secure treatment and pain relief for her child. She was deeply struck by the difference in Theo's experiences to those of her other, non-disabled children who don't face the delays, stigma and barriers that Theo routinely encounters. Theo can't explain pain, or changes to his vision, because he doesn't tend to communicate using speech. Anna knew he was disoriented and in terrible pain, but medical staff described his behaviours in relation to his autism and suggested he was experiencing a 'bad time of year'. Theo's behaviour (his expressions of pain!) became unmanageable and frightening to his younger siblings. He started to receive 2:1 support and couldn't be safely cared for at home. This was an extreme low point for Theo and his whole family.

The hospital health team were concerned about the risk of using a general anaesthetic for Theo's treatment, so took their treatment plan to the Court of Protection in February 2020. Anna first knew about this when she was phoned by the Judge. It was half term. Children were running around. Anna had no idea she was being live streamed in court, and answered the phone in her usual informal, friendly style. But she quickly realised this was a turning point in Theo's journey, as the Judge, Mr Justice Hayden, said:

> For anybody who has had toothache, even delay between now and then looks like an eternity. But this young man, it seems, has been suffering, and significantly so, for nearly five months. This is little short of an outrage. It is indefensible ...
> (England and Wales Court of Protection Decisions v P, 2020)

So, what happened next? Mr Justice Hayden gave weight to Anna and her husband's knowledge of their son. He valued their expertise and ordered that treatment should take place immediately. Fortuitously, Theo's treatment took place just before the country went into the Covid lockdown. He had six teeth removed; his wisdom teeth had been growing in the wrong direction. He also had a bone removed.

Anna says she feels Theo and others with his level of need are the 'forgotten part of society', but also that, as his mum, she was invisible too. When he had his operation, they were given no information about aftercare. It was only three days later, when he started to bleed, that they realised he'd had so many teeth removed and stitches applied. Anna still worries about the long-term health impacts of all the bangs to Theo's head as well as of the trauma experienced by her other children.

So, this is a story about how ordinary stuff – toothache and access to dental treatment – can become cloaked in stigma, discrimination and ultimately threaten people's human rights. For Theo this was a breach of his article 2 rights, because his life was at risk due to the extent of his head injuries; I would argue article 3 because he was left experiencing severe pain for so long; article 5 as Theo's freedoms gradually eroded as his needs increased; and I would also argue article 6 rights (to a fair trial), because of the delay in referring Theo's case to the Court of Protection.

Anna considers the dominant narrative to have been Theo's autism. This prevented him being seen with compassion, as human, and afforded his basic right to health care.

The life expectancy of men with learning disabilities is 66 years: 14 years lower than men in the general population. The life expectancy for women living with learning disabilities is 67 years: 17 years lower than women in the general population (NHS Digital, 2020). As social workers, we need to challenge the discrimination and abuse faced by people with learning disabilities and autism. We also need to face up to and address our role in perpetuating the discrimination of the system. We have a vital role to play in questioning, challenging and working from a social justice and human rights perspective. This means we must be fully aware of the inequalities reported annually by LeDeR (nd) and a succession of Serious Adult Reviews, and we must ensure we meet the Capabilities Statement for Social Workers Working with Adults with Learning Disability (BASW, 2019).

It's essential that social workers understand when urgent escalation to the Court of Protection is needed, such as when life or welfare is at risk and a decision cannot be delayed, as it was in Theo's case. As Mr Justice Hayden remarked, the five months of pain that Theo endured and the delay in bringing the case to the Court of Protection was an indefensible outrage.

Following the operation, Theo instantly improved. Anna said, '*suddenly something lifted*'. Theo now lives on a farm half an hour from his family home. He's enjoying the freedom offered by country life and is learning how to be more independent. Finding this home was another battle for Anna, as she needed to persuade services to recognise months of uncontrollable behaviour as an expression of severe and untreated pain and not as Theo's usual way of being. But that's another story for another time. Theo is now living a good life, in the countryside, with the animals and sense of space he so values.

Enid

Finding out what's most important to someone should be at the heart of any assessment and is essential in ensuring that people's rights are upheld. My next story is about Enid and was told to me by Social Work Apprentice Mary. Mary met Enid when she was asked to assess with a view to Enid returning home from hospital. Enid lived on her own and had no close family. Before being admitted to hospital she'd been living at home without any help, but this had been a struggle. Professionals in the hospital described her as '*not engaging*' and doubted her capacity to make decisions about her care and support needs and where to live.

Enid was 90 years old and during her working life she'd been a glamorous and successful head teacher. But in hospital she was withdrawn, dishevelled and, notably, had very little hair. Enid quietly mentioned to Mary that her wig had been put in the drawer next to her. Mary dried the wig, brushed it and gave it to Enid to wear. The transformation was immediate. Enid's confidence seemed to be restored along with her hair. Once she felt presentable, Enid felt human and could work with Mary to plan her return home.

By tuning in to what mattered to Enid, Mary was able to support her to regain control of her life and return home. When Mary visited her at home, Enid showed her wonderful photos of herself through the years wearing an array of fantastic wigs. Enid's wigs and, therefore, her hair were a cornerstone of her identity, and without recognising this and responding to it she was nearly excluded from making important decisions about her future (article 6) as well as risking her article 8 rights. Without her hair, Enid wasn't herself, and didn't have the self-esteem to participate in fundamental decisions about her life.

Ken

As a prison social worker, Bal strives to bring social work values into the way she works. This is ably demonstrated in the story about her work with Ken.

The prison where Ken has lived for many years updated their bathroom facilities, but the new design was such that Ken went from being able to independently shower to being unable to meet his own personal care needs. When Bal met him, he hadn't had a shower for three years. Recognising his eligible needs under the Care Act 2014, Bal arranged for care staff to accompany him to another wing of the prison that still has the old design bathrooms and where Ken can shower himself. The irony is that Ken showers independently with the right facilities, and he only needs to be accompanied to the facilities. But the fact that the prison staff have been unable to support this means he has eligible care needs and, with help to get to the other wing, Ken is able to shower. This may seem a convoluted way to enable a man to have a shower and Bal is working with the prison to understand how its environment can unintentionally disable.

But it's the *'ordinary stuff'* which Bal does which has the most impact. She talked to me about when she first joined the team and all professional visits happened in the sterile environment of the legal room. Bal feels it's important to see people *'in their homes'* as much as possible, to understand how they are living and impacted by their environment. She gives the people she works with as much choice as possible about where within the prison their social work visits should take place. She also sees the importance of letting people know when she's visiting. Bal makes appointments so people have control and can prepare, and she has a visible presence within the prison so that people can approach her directly. I asked Ken how this approach makes him feel, and he said it gave him a sense of having some choice and feeling like a human, not a number.

Bal says prison strips people of their identity: what they wear, what they do, when to eat, when they have appointments. People have no control over their day-to-day life. She calls people by their names, not their numbers, and asks people to use her name rather than *'miss'* or *'sir'*. Ken says just using first names makes a real difference to anyone in prison. The prison system's barriers between staff and inmates make it hard to build any form of trust. But Bal's use of names removes one small but important barrier.

Our Social Work Code of Ethics, under social justice, identifies we have

> *a duty to challenge social conditions that contribute to oppression, social exclusion, stigma or subjugation, and work towards an inclusive society.*
>
> (BASW, 2021)

This is challenging when we work within structures that don't hold the same values, but Bal's work shows how we can make small changes with big impact by remaining true to our core values. The language we use, being relationship-focused and strengths-based helps people feel valued and respected in the most difficult of circumstances.

Maisie

The final person I spoke to for this chapter was Maisie. I asked her about her experiences of living in a care home during the Covid lockdowns when her human rights were incredibly restricted and, like others living in care homes, she was prevented from seeing her closest family members and loved ones in efforts to preserve her article 2 right to life.

Maisie, who is 94 years old, was wonderful to listen to. She told me about the things that make her feel human: a connection to nature and life outside of the home. She likes to watch squirrels eating nuts from the bird feeder or being chased by a cat who's never quite quick enough. She enjoys watching people walking past on their way to school or work or walking their dogs. She loves socialising with her friends in the home: playing Play Your Cards Right and Bingo, where she'd won some lovely prizes, often as gifts for her family. She enjoys cross-stitch, and making cards for her friends and family, to whom she regularly writes. After a brief stay in hospital, Maisie caught Covid, or 'the germs', and was isolated in a different wing within the care home, where she was stoically concerned for everyone else's safety. It was essential to her that, when everything else was stripped away, she still had these activities in place that connected her to herself and made her feel human.

Maisie's care home made it possible for residents to welcome visitors by introducing a visitor's room with a glass wall in it, an intercom and a separate entrance from the garden so that loved ones didn't need to enter the rest of the home, unless there were circumstances where this was essential, such as when people were nearing the end of their life.

Maisie felt her care home got the balance right. She knew the team worked hard to prevent an outbreak and, apart from Maisie and her friend, they'd been largely successful. Maisie said the residents felt the home's manager did everything she could to protect them, and the visiting process was fair.

Maisie used to have an extensive collection of thimbles. She'd started it when she was 16 years old and had collected thimbles from all around the world. Some had been brought home to her by her husband, who was in the Navy. More recently, she'd added to her collection from holiday travels. These were important to Maisie for many reasons. She proudly told me about the interest her grandson had taken in her collection and how he'd written about them for his school project and cleaned them all individually for her. But, frustratingly, when she'd moved into care, the importance of the thimbles hadn't been recognised, and many had gone missing, so she only had a small part of her collection still with her.

Since becoming a Principal Social Worker, I often miss working directly with people and this was a time when I wished I could have gone back in time and been Maisie's social worker. I hoped I wouldn't have been too under pressure to notice the importance of the thimbles, and to hear her wish to take them to her new home and to be able to ensure that they were packed carefully and taken with her.

On being human and having rights

What makes us human, and therefore the rights we need to protect, are often not the big, dramatic things. They are being able to see a dentist when you're in pain, being able to look the way you want to so that you feel digni-fied and respectable, being called your name and having as much choice as you can or feeling connected to your own history and identity through your belongings. This is the ordinary but precious stuff of life, and it's our role as social workers to notice it, listen, and act when these rights are compromised. When we can see that people are being bundled up, processed, passed through a system without thought of who they are and what they might be striving for, to achieve their own good life, we need to act, question, agitate. Our role is to stand alongside people, strengthen their voice: speak up and speak out, and that for me is social justice.

At an interview recently, a prospective Social Work Apprentice was asked to describe social work. She said she'd taken clothes into hospital to an older woman who no longer had any relatives. This lady said,

Don't ever stop doing what you do, because people like me, need people like you.

Reflections

- What does human rights-based practice mean to you?
- List three elements of the '*ordinary stuff*' of your life and consider how these might this be framed within the context of human rights
- How does social justice feature in your everyday practice?

References

Allen, R (2018) Welcome New Social Workers the World Really Needs You! *Professional Social Work*, September 2018.

BASW (British Association of Social Workers) (2019) Capabilities Statement for Social Workers Working with Adults with Learning Disability. [online] Available at: www.basw.co.uk/resources/capabilities-statement-social-workers-working-adults-learning-disability (accessed 2 November 2022).

BASW (2021) The Code of Ethics for Social Work. [online] Available at: www.basw.co.uk/about-basw/code-ethics (accessed 2 November 2022).

Cottam, H (2018) *Radical Help: How We Can Remake the Relationships Between Us and Revolutionise the Welfare State*. London: Virago Press.

England and Wales Court of Protection Decisions (2020) Cardiff & Vale University Health Board v P [2020] EWCOP 8. [online] Available at: www.bailii.org/ew/cases/EWCOP/2020/8.htm (accessed 2 November 2022).

LeDeR (nd) Annual Reports. [online] Available at: www.leder.nhs.uk/resources/annual-reports (accessed 2 November 2022).

NHS Digital (2020) Health & Care of People with Learning Disabilities, Experimental Statistics: 2018–2019. [online] Available at: https://digital.nhs.uk/data-and-information/publications/statistical/health-and-care-of-people-with-learning-disabilities/experimental-statistics-2018-to-2019/condition-prevalence (accessed 2 November 2022).

Social Care Future (2022) #SocialCareFuture. [online] Available at: https://socialcarefuture.blog (accessed 2 November 2022).

Spreadbury, K and Hubbard, R (2020) The Adult Safeguarding Practice Handbook. Bristol: Policy Press.

CHAPTER 8

DOES SUSTAINABILITY HAVE A PLACE IN SOCIAL WORK?

Tendai Murowe

A strange request

Back in 2019, the local authority where I worked declared a climate emergency. An environmental sustainability department was created and a sustainability strategy was developed. All departments, including Children's Services, were asked to develop a Sustainability Action Plan. I was asked to lead this on behalf of Children's Services. We were in the first Covid lockdown when I asked the following question: *'Given the extreme pressures already faced by Children's Services, is there a place here for environmental sustainability?'* My chapter will share my findings with you and challenge you to consider how sustainability is built into your practice.

In my local authority, the children's social work department had never explicitly included sustainability actions within its own operations, relying instead on corporate efforts to tackle climate change, so I assumed my colleagues would question how social workers could relate to the council's agenda for sustainability. We don't run council buildings or drive council cars, and the pandemic had slashed our home-to-work mileage. The Children's Services Department had previously scored lowest in our council's staff survey for working flexibly and at home; we were reluctant to leave the office and work remotely. Despite the cost in transport, we wanted to get out there with children and families and then be back in the office with colleagues where we could receive supervision and support. My impression was that sustainability is a personal rather than professional matter for social workers.

But when I spoke to colleagues, I was immediately struck by the engagement and enthusiasm in the room. Colleagues spoke passionately about environmental sustainability and had lots of ideas on its implementation. It was refreshing to see how busy colleagues wanted to take on the environmental sustainability agenda and I decided to explore this further and to find out more about how social workers regard environmental sustainability in their practice.

What is it, then?

For many of us in the developed world, sustainability and environmental impacts are distant issues with little impact on our everyday life. We hear it on the news, and we ignore the faintly alarming reports about glaciers melting and temperatures rising.

However, it's time to pay more attention. For example, the reported 0.5°C increase in temperature since 2000 has caused forests to lose their natural defences against fire, insects and windstorms. This threatens almost 60 per cent of Europe's forests (Forzieri et al, 2021). There are frightening stories of the reduction in biodiversity. For example, climate change is impacting the existence of bees, a species crucial to agriculture as it impacts 90 per cent of wild plants and 70 per cent of leading global crops (WWF, 2019). A study of the East of England region published in 2019, undertaken by WWF, found that 11 per cent were threatened, 7 per cent were regionally extinct and 14 per cent were of conservation concern. This threatens global food security.

Still, this could feel quite distant for many of us who live in urban or semi-rural environments of the developed world. It may seem far away to those of us who always have food to eat and an economy that can sustain us. But it's current and fresh for those who rely on the climate for their livelihood and who regularly experience hunger, floods and drought. Closer to home, we often forget the impact of environmental concerns such as pollution on our health and well-being. DEFRA (2021) highlighted that poor air quality on pre-existing respiratory health conditions (particularly on the elderly and infants) is the biggest environmental risk to health in the UK. In the first case of its kind, a UK court made a ruling linking 9-year-old Ella Kissi-Debrah's untimely death with her lifelong residence near highly polluting roads in her hometown of Lewisham (Mavrokefalidis, 2022). This shocking case highlights the impact of the environment on health. Air quality may also be associated with poor mental health. Exposure to the most common pollutants in London for children aged 12 years has been found to be significantly associated with increased odds of major depressive disorder at age 18 (Roberts et al, 2019). Adolescents need adequate and safe housing with clean neighbourhoods free from litter and pollution.

Like many, I've been vaguely conscious of these issues. However, once I started this work, I was amazed by how much sustainability impinged on my consciousness. My recent visit to Norway on a cruise brought home the increasing melting of icecaps in that region, which, while a spectacular sight for a visiting tourist, are an indication of the rising global temperatures. On my visits to family in sub-Saharan Africa, I am struck by how much later the rains now fall. The first rains heralding the rainy season used to arrive in October, and now it is nearly Christmas before animals can expect to have grass growing and water in the rivers and dams. The pain and suffering this causes always brings home to me the reality of climate change. The impacts of drought and floods and the devastation this brings to beloved communities and environments are always heart-breaking.

What do social workers understand about sustainability?

I asked social work colleagues what they understand about sustainability and it was heartening to hear how aware and engaged they are. Everyone asked understood the term 'environmental sustainability' and colleagues spoke about recycling, plastics, pollution, green spaces and climate change, among other topics.

Most questioned had an understanding of global sustainability issues such as climate change, energy efficiency, green gases and the connection of their personal actions such as driving, flying, use of plastics and management of waste. We may not formally talk about sustainability in Children's Services but we're aware of it. Social workers mentioned developing understanding from family members, media coverage and activists such as the Swedish student Greta Thunberg. Some grew up with environmentally aware parents who were passionate about sustainability and this had helped to shape their values. All talked about concern for future generations, and the impact of personal actions on the environment. There was no mention, however, of social work education having contributed to their knowledge or consciousness about sustainability issues.

I asked colleagues what actions they take personally at home that are sustainable. All could mention at least three things. Almost all mentioned recycling, sustainable travel and managing waste. The level of commitment varied from those that just did these activities because the law requires it to those consciously taking action to sustain the environment. It was obvious that all were highly conscious of the importance of environmental sustainability and their desire to do more to contribute to this.

But, notably, no immediate links were made between climate change and the lives of the children and families that we support. There was no connection made between lawlessness and deprived neighbourhoods or disease and waste in the streets. There was no mention of overcrowded houses or the lack of green, outdoor spaces for children and young people to play and develop safely. And there was no word about our responsibility as a profession to contribute to this agenda. I wondered whether we were so focused on dealing with the symptoms of societal problems and the difficulties families have in adjusting that we've forgotten to take a systemic view of problems families can experience and to consider how the environment contributes to this.

What can social workers do in the workplace to implement more sustainable approaches?

The social workers I spoke to had six clear ideas about how sustainability can be built into day-to-day practice within the workplace.

1. Individual behaviour change

Sustainable behaviour starts with individual behaviour change and it's this that leads to cultural shift. Policies can steer but culture is key, and we each need to take responsibility for our part in this. My colleagues had ideas about how culture change can be promoted through away-days, team meetings and workshops to promote the importance of sustainability and to encourage engagement and ownership. Team Sustainability Champions, who carry out team activities and keep the sustainability agenda alive, can be appointed to highlight opportunities for sustainable behaviour. There's merit in introducing smaller changes that people can manage, for example in travelling habits such as using low emission cars or walking rather than driving short journeys.

2. It's about values

Social workers should lead by example. Leaders of organisations and teams should clearly articulate sustainability expectations. Strategies should be co-created alongside the children and families being supported as they will be impacted by any changes in practice. People change their behaviours when they share the values being presented and can take ownership in the strategy. Busy social workers need to see that their behaviour change is having an impact. There's a place here for metrics; how many fewer disposable coffee cups are going into landfill now that the council has become plastic-free? How much has the department's carbon consumption been reduced through use of electric cars?

What was missing from my conversations with colleagues was any reference to social work values contributing to our understanding of sustainability. There's currently no mention of environmental sustainability or values in the Professional Standards for Social Work in England (SWE, 2019) and there's no formal expectation that social workers should build environmental consideration or sustainability into their practice. Similarly, environmental concerns don't feature in SWE Professional Standards for Social Work Education.

Employers of social workers aren't performing any better. Core training and development offers in most Children's Services departments show no consideration of how environmental sustainability should be addressed as part of social work practice.

Social Work England, social work employers and social work educators need to include sustainability needs in professional and educational standards and curricula as well as continuing professional development frameworks for social workers as a matter of urgency.

3. It's about the ease

Child protection work is busy and there are in-built barriers to being able to behave in sustainable ways. Poor IT systems and a presentism culture make remote working difficult, and while this changed dramatically during the Covid-19 pandemic, managers' attitudes to remote working are again having an impact on social workers' ability to think sustainably. When in the office, recycling bins should be conveniently situated and clearly marked. Electric vehicles should be available as part of the car lease or loan arrangements and social workers should be equipped with the IT and furniture needed to work comfortably and more flexibly.

Social workers I spoke to said that if sustainable behaviours were made easier, they would perform them. If there's public transport, it will be used. If there are recycling bins, these will be used. If children are living close to their homes rather than 200 miles away, there will be more sustainable travel. Employers of social workers should consider how they can make sustainable behaviour easier. Often the lack of local resources, schools, homes for children or accessibility to services for families makes thinking local very difficult. *'Think local'* should be a key consideration when *'growing your own social workers'* and incentives should be in place for people to work more locally.

4. It's about the money

Sustainability alternatives can be costly and should be subsidised. Locally sourced vegan food should be available in work canteens and promotional activities in the workplace such as *'meatless Thursdays'* should be encouraged.

There were suggestions about educating people on sustainable eating by offering free recipes and cooking lessons. For families, eating sustainably can be expensive and financial incentives need to be introduced. This might include subsidising and lowering tax on sustainably sourced products and lower business rates for services providing sustainable goods. I remember as a child that there were huge incentives for recycling, as you received a discount on the cost of your milk or bottled drinks if you returned an empty bottle. This may feel like a stretch from day-to-day social work practice, but many of us work for influential local authorities with tremendous purchasing power and influence over the local market. It's for us to exercise our influence as employees to effect changes in local policy.

When building support packages for families, we need to consider the most sustainable ways of doing this. Local authorities often struggle with the cost of home to school travel, but where this is a safe option we should consider alternatives such as bicycles. Looked-after children could be taught bike safety and provided with bikes. Local authorities must ensure public transport is available and affordable, and infrastructure for safe biking must be in place. Incentives such as these would attract more sustainable ways of living for families and social workers.

Decisions which are good for children might also have environmental benefits and offer organisational advantages. Social workers in management roles must form their decisions to benefit both the child and the environment. For example, children in the care of the local authority being returned to live locally (from other local authorities where they currently reside) serves a dual purpose of being extremely good for the child while at the same time cutting both carbon and financial costs of travel for staff and families who visit them and for home-to-school transport. A truly child-focused and sustainability-oriented manager can find these wins whenever possible.

5. It's about co-creation

We know young people cite climate change as the top of their list of concerns and this was confirmed in an unpublished 2019 survey carried out by Coram Voice among young people looked after by my local authority.

Social workers should listen to the young people we support and lead on sustainability by example. We need to push from within to harness the wide reach of our employing local authorities and demand they lead on the approach to sustainability taken by residents, schools and businesses. Social work activism is important for our profession, and when being consulted by our authorities we should advocate for this, and support our young people to get their voices heard.

6. It's about relationships

Young people are very conscious of the environment. I recently worked alongside a group of young people as part of a project on inclusion. They spoke passionately about how important it is for them to take part in activities for the betterment of society. This is an important message for social workers and there are many ways we can respond. A local Participation

Team supported young people in the care of my local authority to undertake a tree-planting day as part of a sustainability initiative. The young people were passionate about this project and committed to its success. We know about the connection between green spaces and good mental health (Barton and Rogerson, 2017) and about the poorer health outcomes for people without easy access to green spaces (Maas et al, 2009). Social workers need to explicitly build this understanding into our practice and recognise the impact of environmental pressures for the families living in concrete, urban areas with noise pollution and overcrowding. Environmentally sustainable activities such as the tree-planting project mentioned above can provide options for engaging and building relationships with children and families. The impact of being outside and working to secure the tree's future together offers a common, creative and energising purpose. Empathy, compassion and genuine connections with young people and their families allows for a true understanding of the constraints that the environment can bring for many families.

So, should social workers be worried about sustainability?

Let's be clear about this; sustainability must be the concern of every social worker. Our mandate lies within the International Federation of Social Work's Global Definition of Social Work (IFSW, 2014). Social work is 'a practice-based profession' which 'promotes social change and social development'. Social development aims for 'sustainable development' which is multi-system and inter-sectorial.

There are different approaches to thinking about sustainability in social work. 'Green social work' addresses the challenge of it being poorer people who bear the brunt of environmental degradation (Powers et al, 2018). 'Eco-social work' (Norton, 2011) considers the 'person in environment', the relationships between people and their environment. Currently, sustainable and environmental social work is significantly better developed globally and in developing countries than in the UK. There have been some international responses to sustainability and social work, for example, as the third agenda item in the Global Agenda for Social Work and Social Development: Commitment to Action, 'Working toward Environmental

Sustainability' (IFSW et al, 2012). However, by their scarcity, these responses feel distant and half-hearted.

This is a start, but we need to go much further and the UK urgently needs to pick up speed. Social Work England, professional associations such as BASW, social work educators and social work employers must lead the way in creating shared values around environmental sustainability for social workers. And each individual social worker must take up their own agency to lead the way towards environmental sustainability within their own sphere of influence.

Social work in the developed world tends to be more concerned with individuals and their families than with communities, and the stringent policies and guidance have eroded the flexibility that came with community-based social work. This has distracted us from the very real impact of the environment on individuals and communities. We struggle to recognise the true impact of poverty and the environment on the ability of families to keep children safe and we've failed to take up a leadership role in tackling environmental threats to the safety of children.

Social work is a relational profession, and the environment is important for the people we help. When we consider people's environments in assessments, in our planning and in our interventions, we are working with the whole person instead of narrowly focusing on the presenting problems. Sustainability also offers opportunities for engagement and direct work, and we may be surprised, once we ask the questions, how important the environment is to children and families that we work with.

So, does sustainability have a place in social work?

Social workers must learn to see the link between the problems faced by families and the environment within which they live. This will help us connect with families, as recognition is given to the impact of environment as a stressor and barrier to well-being. It also helps build relationships with young people, who are already very conscious of environmental issues.

Sustainability must be *'business as usual'* for social workers. It can't be an *'add-on'*. Social workers want to talk about and act on sustainability, and its importance for future generations and this must be supported by our professional associations, our employers, our educators and our regulator. But the social work profession is a body of autonomous individuals and it is for each of us to act now. We must ask ourselves, *'What can I do to make my practice more environmentally sustainable?'*.

Reflections

- How can we as social workers incorporate sustainability in our practice?

- How might we use collective action to influence sustainability agendas in social work education and training?

- To what extent are environmental concerns shared with the people we support and how might our common experience impact our approach to practice?

References

Barton, J and Rogerson, M (2017) The Importance of Greenspace for Mental Health. Cambridge.org. [online] Available at: www.cambridge.org/core/journals/bjpsych-international/article/importance-of-greenspace-for-mental-health/EEFD7077B5E3823086FB187FABE535C2# (accessed 10 August 2022).

DEFRA (2021) Annual Report 2020 Issue 2 Online Viewer – Defra, UK. [online] Available at: https://uk-air.defra.gov.uk/library/annualreport/viewonline?year=2020_issue_2#report_pdf (accessed 9 August 2022).

Forzieri, G, Girardello, M, Ceccherini, G, Spinoni, J, Feyen, L, Hartmann, H, Beck, P, Camps-Valls, G, Chirici, G, Mauri, A and Cescatti, A (2021) Emergent Vulnerability to Climate-Driven Disturbances in European Forests. *Nature Communications*, 12(1081). https://doi.org/10.1038/s41467-021-21399-7.

International Federation of Social Workers (IFSW) (2014) Global Definition of Social Work. [online] Available at: www.ifsw.org/what-is-social-work/global-definition-of-social-work (accessed 14 November 2022).

International Federation of Social Workers, International Association of Schools of Social Work et al (2012) The Global Agenda for Social Work and Social Development: Commitment to Action. [online] Available at: www.ifsw.org/what-is-social-work/global-definition-of-social-work/ (accessed 14 November 2022).

Maas, J, Verheij, R A, de Vries, S, Spreeuwenberg, P, Schellevis, F G and Groenewegen, P P (2009) Morbidity is Related to a Green Living Environment. *Journal of Epidemiology and Community Health*, 63(12): 967–73.

Mavrokefalidis, D (2022) Ella Kissi-Debrah: The Story of a Canary in a Coal Mine – Energy Live News. *Energy Live News*. [online] Available at: www.energylivenews.com/2021/06/17/ella-kissi-debrah-the-story-of-a-canary-in-a-coal-mine/ (accessed 10 August 2022).

Norton, C L (2011) Social Work and the Environment: An Ecosocial Approach. *International Journal of Social Welfare*, 21: 299–308.

Roberts, S, Arseneault, L, Barratt, B, Beevers, S, Danese, A, Odgers, C, Moffitt, T, Reuben, A, Kelly, F and Fisher, H (2019) Exploration of NO_2 and $PM_{2.5}$ Air Pollution and Mental Health Problems Using High-Resolution Data in London-Based Children from a UK Longitudinal Cohort Study. *Psychiatry Research*, 272: 8–17.

Powers, M C F, Willett, J, Mathias, J and Hayward, A (2018) Green Social Work for Environmental Justice: Implications for International Social Workers. In Dominelli, L (ed) *The Routledge Handbook of Green Social Work* (pp 74–84). Abingdon: Routledge.

SWE (2019) *Professional Standards*. Social Work England. [online] Available at: www.socialworkengland.org.uk/standards/professional-standards/ (accessed 12 October 2022).

WWF (2019) Bees Under Siege from Habitat Loss, Climate Change and Pesticides. [online] Available at: www.wwf.org.uk/sites/default/files/2019-05/EofE%20bee%20report%202019%20FINAL_17MAY2019.pdf (accessed 9 August 2022).

CHAPTER 9

POVERTY AND THE NEED FOR RADICAL RELATIONAL PRACTICE

Lisa Aldridge

For Mum

Introduction

I am honoured to have an opportunity to contribute to this book through writing a chapter on poverty. As for many people who move into helping professions, childhood experiences motivated me to do something that would both create change for myself and make a difference to others. I have clear memories of growing up in our council house in a village outside of Bristol at times when my mum, as our breadwinner, would struggle to find money to make ends meet – this was as a result of low-paid work, my father being in the fire brigade strikes in the 1970s and then his being in and out of mental health hospitals for a number of years. My mum would eat jam sandwiches so that my sister and I could eat proper meals. I was lucky. I never went hungry. Decades later, families are continuing to have to go without the very basics that they need to survive: quality food, housing and heating.

The context of the current cost-of-living crisis means that, more than ever, social workers must be sensitive and responsive to the presence of poverty. Poverty is a consistent contextual factor for many of the children and families we support, but to what extent does our practice acknowledge poverty as a structurally influencing factor? Do we pay enough attention to the impact of poverty and do we recognise the role of social work in addressing it?

In this chapter I'll explore the potential for poverty-informed social work practice and will conclude that to challenge the structural, address the practical and respond to the emotional impact of poverty, social work should develop a poverty-aware relational approach from its own radical roots.

What does poverty look like in the UK today?

The Joseph Rowntree Foundation (JRF) defines poverty as living on 60 per cent or below of the median income and not being able to afford certain essential items and activities. According to its Poverty Profile (Joseph Rowntree Foundation, 2022a), 14.5 million people in the UK are living in poverty. This includes 4.3 million children and 2.1 million pensioners.

The Child Poverty Action Group (CPAG, nda) report that, in the UK, 46 per cent of children of global majority families and 26 per cent of children in white British families live in poverty; 49 per cent of children living in poverty are growing up in single parent families; 75 per cent of children growing up in poverty live in a household where at least one person works, demonstrating that poverty is not only an issue only for families who are out of work and supported through benefits.

We need to talk about poverty. Analysis undertaken by the JRF (Joseph Rowntree Foundation, 2022b) found that April 2022 marked the greatest fall in the value of the basic rate of out-of-work benefit in 50 years. Their survey of people living in deep poverty (40 per cent or below of median income) found 5.2 million low-income households where family members had cut down, skipped meals or gone hungry because there wasn't enough money for food. A total of 3.2 million households had been unable to adequately heat their home and 4.6 million were in arrears on at least one bill. Ten years of cuts and freezes to benefits, including the introduction of the benefit cap in 2013 and its lowering in 2016, followed by the two-child limit introduced for children born after 2017, particularly targets larger families who are most vulnerable to being in deep poverty.

Impact of poverty on children and families

As well as rendering families unable to pay for rent, bills, food, clothing and other necessities, poverty can create disadvantages in terms of health outcomes, life expectancy, psychological well-being, mental health, educational outcomes and lifetime opportunities for children.

CPAG (ndb) describes how surviving on a low or inadequate income impacts upon parental stress, family dynamics and relationships. Poverty can impact children's friendships (bullying, access to school trips, being embarrassed to bring friends home), their mental health (anxiety, stress, worry about parents, insecurity and sense of hopelessness) and their aspirations and outcomes. Children who have lived in persistent poverty in their first seven years have cognitive development scores of an average 20 per cent below other children.

Parents experiencing poverty may have to take multiple jobs and/or shift work, impacting upon the extent to which they are able to supervise older children. Parents may experience stress, depression or other mental health problems as a result of structural oppression, and this may impact upon their parenting capacity. Children who experience poverty may feel different and even ashamed. Older children may want to help their parents make ends meet or they may want to be able to buy clothing or other items that increase their social status, rendering them vulnerable to exploitation during adolescence.

Children and families social work

Within social work, many of the families we support are on low incomes, often living in poor quality, temporary or overcrowded accommodation. Many were struggling to make ends meet before the Covid-19 pandemic but are finding things even harder now. The Child Welfare Inequalities Project (Bywaters and Featherstone, 2020) found that deprivation was a major factor in children coming into care and being supported through Child Protection Plans. Poverty is a pervasive and interwoven factor creating a context for neglect, interacting with other needs and risks such as parental mental health, domestic abuse, substance misuse and extra-familial harm.

What can we do?

There are practical steps we can take to support families to maximise their income through access to benefits, debt management and income maximisation. In my local authority, the schemes we routinely explore include the following:

- the Healthy Start programme which provides pregnant women and parents with children under 4 years of age with fruit, milk and vitamins;

- local food banks and/or Community Food shops – the latter of which request a donation of up to £5 to receive around £20 worth of culturally appropriate food;

- free school meals – families on low incomes, including families with no recourse to public funds, can be supported to make an application;

- school uniform grant applications should be encouraged and families made aware that this is not dependent upon access to free school meals;

- council tax rebates;

- 15 hours of free childcare and additional food vouchers for holiday breaks for children aged 2 and above if families are in receipt of benefits or are working but receiving a low income;

- short-term resources currently available include the government-funded Household Support Fund, distributing funds via councils to residents with greatest need, and food vouchers distributed by voluntary and community services to families with children under age 5 years.

Children supported through statutory Children and Families social work can be provided with financial support and resources through Section 17 of the Children Act 1989. So urgent items such as children's clothing, bedding, food vouchers or money for gas or electric prepayment metres can be provided to ensure that children are fed, clothed and warm, while other longer-term resources are identified. Families receiving direct payments for children with disabilities may redirect some of these resources to meet immediate practical needs such as for food or heating. Practitioners can make charity and grant applications to support families in purchasing furniture, white goods and for help with the costs of paint for redecorating. It's every social worker's responsibility to be aware of national and local schemes that offer material and practical assistance to people experiencing poverty.

Radical roots

Of course, social work is more than signposting to schemes. The relationship that contains our practice is the means through which we engage with the meaning of families' experiences. It must be anti-oppressive, anti-discriminatory, anti-racist and trauma-informed with a clear aim to support families to become independent in their parenting. But we must learn from our history. Social work's historic focus on social justice gave way to the Thatcherite-informed demand for individual responsibility. And now we seem to overlook our role to intervene in structural factors such as poverty, racism and inequality in favour of insistence upon individual responsibility. The expectation seems to be that people should be able to individually overcome wider structural forces to create the changes they need in their lives.

Of course, it's easier to work with a single family than with a structurally problematic society, but if we are to have meaningful impact social workers should be aware of which groups of people are most likely to be in poverty and should advocate a structural, systemic and intersectional approach to their support. We might feel limited in our ability to change deeply embedded structural factors. How effective can we be in the face of the current government's policies on benefits and minimum wages, or upon the impact of inflation, food prices and unregulated capitalism that allows companies to achieve billions of pounds in oil profits at the same time as we're experiencing a fuel crisis and astronomical fuel prices? But we do have agency as citizens, voters, campaigners and activists and we should take every opportunity to speak out against poverty and highlight and support the work of anti-poverty campaigners such as Jack Monroe (TED Talks, 2016) or, within our own profession, Dominic Watters (Pierro, 2022).

We can learn much from our radical social work roots to understand oppression in the context of social and economic structures instead of locating problems in the individuals who are oppressed. A radical social work approach to a family in poverty will include: (i) an understanding that the family's difficulties are likely to be located within broader systemic and structural failings; (ii) positioning ourselves alongside the family in their struggle for social justice; and (iii) direct action – campaigning/mobilising to dismantle and overcome the structural failings that deposit disadvantage onto marginalised sections of our communities.

Radical hope

Krumer-Nevo (2020) promotes the importance of social work in the dismantling of the structural oppression caused by poverty. Her Poverty Aware Social Work Paradigm conceives poverty as a violation of human rights. Reduced material capital (money), social capital (education, access to health) and symbolic capital (stigmatisation, discrimination and *othering*) are consistent features of the lived experience of people who live in persistent poverty. The Poverty Aware Paradigm builds upon our radical roots as it demands:

- acknowledgement of poverty as a social injustice;
- transformation in the way social workers perceive, speak and write about the people we support; and
- solidarity and positioning of ourselves alongside families to resist poverty and create change.

But the Poverty Aware Social Work Paradigm also highlights an essential element to our practice in its positioning of rights-based practice within relationship-based practice. Key to understanding the experience of poverty is understanding the emotional pain it creates while respecting the ways families act to resist it. This demands appreciation of people's knowledge and expertise over their own lives and relational connection for authenticity.

Saar-Heiman and Gupta (2020) build upon Krumer-Nevo's work in their presentation of a Poverty Aware Paradigm for Child Protection. They emphasise that parents and children engaged in the Child Protection system deserve better and note how feelings of powerlessness and shame can be associated with poverty and expressed through subtle micro-aggressions by professionals which can in turn influence assessments and interventions that follow.

Relational radicals

As social workers, we all should be aware and angry about the existence of poverty. We should locate our agency and take action to resist its wider structural causes. The power of the systemic injustice of poverty should be acknowledged in our work to overcome its impact and our practice should steer clear of any suggestion of blame for individuals. Social work is personal as well as political and the genuine connection of a relational approach is key to creating change with and for children and families.

If you've found this chapter useful, start discussions with your colleagues and managers – plan together what you need to do as a collective to intervene into issues of poverty through individual practice, as a service and as an organisation. Engage your senior leaders to ensure that poverty-informed practice is firmly located within your approach to social work and practice model. Take a rights-based and relational approach to stand in solidarity with children and families impacted by poverty. Make change.

Reflections

- What is your approach to dialogue with families experiencing poverty and how well do you appreciate and reflect their attempts to resist poverty?

- How do you present the cause and impact of poverty within your assessments?

- What have you included in your intervention plan to address structural oppression including poverty and racism to create change for children and families?

References

Bywaters, P and Featherstone, B (2020) *The Child Welfare Inequalities Project: Final Report*. University of Huddersfield. [online] Available at: https://pure.hud.ac.uk/en/publications/the-child-welfare-inequalities-project-final-report (accessed 14 November 2022).

Child Poverty Action Group (nda) Child Poverty Facts and Figures. [online] Available at: https://cpag.org.uk/child-poverty/child-poverty-facts-and-figures (accessed 8 November 2022).

Child Poverty Action Group (ndb) The Effects of Poverty. [online] Available at: https://cpag.org.uk/child-poverty/effects-poverty (accessed 8 November 2022).

Joseph Rowntree Foundation (2022a) UK Poverty 2022, The Essential Guide to Understanding Poverty in the UK, Joseph Rowntree Foundation. [online] Available at: www.jrf.org.uk/report/uk-poverty-2022 (accessed 8 November 2022).

Joseph Rowntree Foundation (2022b) Diving Beneath the Surface of Poverty. [online] Available at: www.jrf.org.uk/blog/diving-beneath-surface-poverty (accessed 8 November 2022).

Krumer-Nevo, M (2020) *Radical Hope: Poverty-Aware Practice for Social Work*. Bristol: Policy Press.

Pierro, L (2022) It's Taking a Deprived Single Dad to Highlight Issues of Food Insecurity. *Community Care*. [online] Available at: www.communitycare.co.uk/2022/03/24/its-taking-a-deprived-single-dad-to-highlight-issues-of-food-insecurity/#.YzFReHbMK5c (accessed 8 November 2022).

Saar-Heiman, Y and Gupta, A (2020) The Poverty-Aware Paradigm for Child Protection: A Critical Framework for Policy and Practice. *The British Journal of Social Work*, 50(4): 1167–84.

TED Talks (2016) Time to Make a Difference. Jack Monroe TEDxWhitehall Women. [online] Available at: https://youtu.be/ueew8giHXM4 (accessed 8 November 2022).

CHAPTER 10

ANTI-RACIST LEADERSHIP

Sara Taylor

Introduction

What does it really mean to be an anti-racist leader? This question is central to social workers in leadership roles and to the profession itself. It's something I've been grappling with since the murder of George Floyd brought about a change in the fabric of our organisation through a new focus on understanding the impact of racism and how to address it. In this chapter, I will explore and describe what becoming (or attempting to become) an anti-racist leader has looked like for me as a white senior leader within a local authority children's social care service.

Exploring difference

To lead in an anti-racist way, we need good understanding of our own values, levels of privilege and power. Understanding difference and sameness is often explored through the Social Graces (Burnham, 2012) (see Figure 10.1). This helpful acronym describes social and personal identity and how people are afforded different levels of power and privilege depending on their position. Using the Social Graces in our work allows us to open up dialogue and understanding about privilege and power and how we position ourselves in relation to aspects of our own experience such as race, ethnicity, class, education and gender.

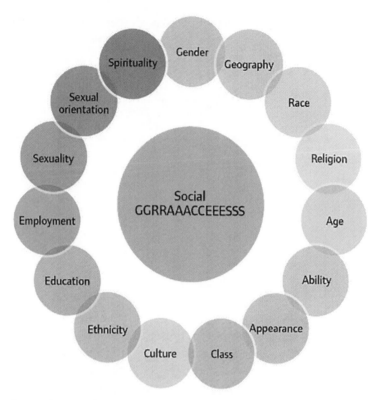

Figure 10.1 Social GGRRAAACCEEESSS (Burnham, 2012).

It's important therefore to state that I am a white British woman born in the 1960s, and from the start of the anti-racist work in my organisation I have been very aware of my position in relation to race, ethnicity and culture. I recognise my privilege as one who does not experience racism. I've reflected on my own background and working-class upbringing where racist attitudes and beliefs were often articulated. I've benefited from the opportunities and education which enabled me to reflect on the values in my own upbringing and choose to take a different path. I'm part of the senior management team in my local authority and I see the leadership in our organisation doesn't reflect our local population or workforce demographic. This adds complexity to an already multi-layered area of practice but one which as leaders in our profession we can't ignore. I have frequently said throughout the process of the development of our anti-racist practice that *'this is the work and however difficult it is, it has to be done'.*

The need for change

The murder of George Floyd drew sharp focus on the need for change nationally, internationally and within my local authority. This sentiment had long been verbalised by global majority colleagues but, in the wake of George Floyd's murder, white colleagues were also being called to action. I work in an inner London borough children's social care service. Our local population is diverse and multicultural with a variety of different nationalities and more than 170 spoken languages. Approximately a quarter of the population are children and young people and a third of these live in poverty. A total of 68 per cent of children and young people identify as black or global majority, with the two largest groups being Black African (20 per cent) and Black Caribbean (17 per cent). Global majority is defined as:

> ... a collective term that first and foremost speaks to and encourages those so-called, to think of themselves as belonging to the majority on planet earth. It refers to people who are Black, African, Asian, Brown, dual-heritage, indigenous to the global south, and or, have been racialised as 'ethnic minorities'. Globally these groups currently represent approximately eighty per cent (80%) of the world's population, making them the global majority now, and with current growth rates, notwithstanding the Covid-19 pandemic, they are set to remain so for the foreseeable future.
>
> (Campbell-Stevens, 2020)

The social care workforce in my local authority is 57 per cent global majority staff. It was evident from the strength of feeling from both black and white staff that the time for change was overdue. Our work started with what we called A Series of Conversations.

A Series of Conversations

As a senior leadership team, we were aware of the need to respond to the murder of George Floyd and to the emotional impact on our workforce.

I recall thinking long and hard in 2020 about how to construct a communication that conveyed what we, an all-white senior leadership group, wanted to share with the workforce about this tragic event and how we intended to respond. I read with interest a recent blog by a social worker manager who was describing how her local authority approached anti-racist practice.

> For me, it started with National Pet Week 2020. George Floyd had just been murdered. The Local Authority where I worked had not sent out an email acknowledging his murder, but was able to send an all-user email asking people to send in pictures of their loved pets.
>
> (Ziregbe, 2022)

I'm not saying my organisation got it right. But I am saying we spent time and emotional energy thinking about how we should communicate with our staff and the wider workforce. On reflection, that was probably the start of my journey into a greater understanding of what being an ally to global majority colleagues really means.

The Series of Conversations were set up as open meetings over eight months. There was no agenda and no obligation to share or speak. It was an attempt to create a space to start the conversation about the impact of racism and about what needed to happen for our organisation to become authentically anti-racist. I led these sessions and tried to create a space where colleagues could talk openly about their experiences and what needed to change. I recall my feelings of discomfort when experiences of racism were shared, combined with an overwhelming feeling that I didn't really know what to do with the information. Although attendees were a diverse group in terms of people's race, age, gender and jobs, it was largely global majority colleagues who spoke. I felt out of place and unsure about what to say and what words to use. I found it hard to be confronted with the rawness of the experiences of racism described. I felt I had always known racism happened, but it seemed unbelievable to me that colleagues were spoken to and treated in the ways being described. As the sessions progressed it became clear that our global majority colleagues had shared enough. Racism was their daily, lived experience. People no longer wanted to talk, they wanted action. And so, the Anti-Racist Network Group found its beginnings.

The Anti-Racist Network Group

The Anti-Racist Network Group is for all staff together to create a vision for an actively anti-racist children's social care service. The group has written an anti-racist statement and action plan and provided space for colleagues to think together. Although I initially sought to develop anti-discriminatory and anti-racist practice within our service, I soon realised that our starting point had to be becoming actively anti-racist in our thinking.

I had begun to fully understand the pervasive nature of racism as part of the day-to-day experience of global majority people and the need for anti-racism to be our starting point. I recognise there are many other groups who experience discrimination and oppression. There's also the concept of 'intersectionality' which draws attention to how 'mutually reinforcing systems of structural and situational inequalities' affect people's experiences (Barnard, 2021, p 5). I'm hopeful that our anti-racist work will lead to further conversations about difference and extend to anti-oppressive and anti-discriminatory thinking and actions with a focus on inclusivity.

Under the surface

One consequence of the group being formed has been the surfacing of experiences and emotions that previously remained hidden. Burnham (2012) refers to what is voiced and unvoiced and visible or not visible in relation to the Social Graces. This can be applied to the functioning of the organisation where, ideally, issues of difference would be located in the visible and voiced quadrant. Initially, I wondered whether experiences of racism and difference had been hidden in the unvoiced and invisible area, yet to be articulated and seen. But I came to understand that much of the unvoiced emotion was keenly felt by global majority colleagues. It was that, as a white member of the leadership team, I'd been shielded from recognising the impact of racism by white privilege.

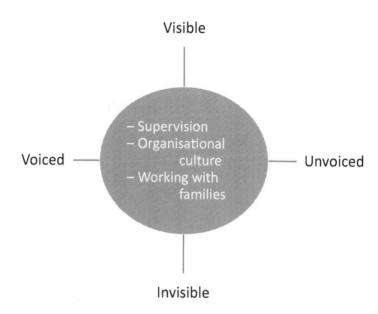

Visible

Voiced — — Unvoiced

- Supervision
- Organisational culture
- Working with families

Invisible

Figure 10.2 Making the Social GGRRAAACCEEESSS visible (from Burnham, 2012).

Psychodynamic thinking as applied to organisations tells us that much of its functioning is beneath the surface and manifests in unconscious actions and behaviours. Menzies Lyth (1959) refers to the idea of socially structured defences in organisations. This means ways of working and organisational structures are put in place to defend against anxiety but can instead serve to increase anxiety and defensiveness. This can result in denial, avoidance and minimisation as well as a lack of organisational containment.

This has meant workers have been unable to acknowledge racism. Global majority staff have been unable to speak out about the need to improve their career development opportunities and these conversations have only recently started to take place through improvements in professional development supervision and expanding opportunities for global majority staff to undertake leadership development programmes.

As we've continued with our anti-racist work, more issues have come to the surface and the leadership team has been confronted with critiques of organisational processes which fail to be anti-racist and with examples of organisational racism. We aim to learn and grow and have taken care to explore all situations, to engage in the difficult conversations and to be vulnerable when we weren't sure, as this example from practice illustrates:

> In discussing an assessment with her supervisor, a social worker who identified as Black African had been asked whether English was her first language. The social worker was upset by the comment which she experienced as a micro-aggression. No concerns had previously been raised about her practice and she was a competent, experienced social worker. The social worker was able to share her experience with a colleague and a meeting was held with the social worker and her manager to discuss the issue and reflect on the learning. The line manager recognised she had made an incorrect assumption about the social worker and needed to approach the discussion about the quality of the assessment from a more curious and open position. The social worker's experience was validated and agreement reached about how the line manager and social worker would try to work together in the future in an actively anti-racist way.

My learning has been on the importance of listening to the experiences of global majority staff and being proactive in our response when issues are raised. To become an anti-racist and anti-oppressive organisation, the conditions must be created to enable challenge and reflection. The Anti-Racist Network Group is an important part of creating such a culture shift. The group continues to develop and is creating an action plan focusing on three key areas: (i) practice with children and families, (ii) partnerships and (iii) workforce development. One significant learning from the Anti-Racist Network Group has been that global majority colleagues need their own space to come together. So we've recently established a safe space for global majority staff to share experiences and learning. This is led by global majority managers across children's social care.

Committing to anti-racist practice

When the Series of Conversations started, the senior leadership team recognised the need to work on anti-racist practice as a team. As a group of leaders, we embarked on a series of reflective learning sessions to increase our understanding of the impact of racism both in our group and the wider workforce. This has been challenging and emotionally demanding but it's been important for us as a management group to work together on a common understanding for anti-racism and to show leadership and commitment to this.

We've now set out our social work vision and values for how we want to work with children and families. These include supporting families to be the experts in their situation, keeping children within their family networks wherever safe and possible and respecting that all children, young people and families are different. If we're to understand what's important to children and families, we need to challenge our own assumptions and bias about culture, ethnicity and race. Social justice is at the heart of our practice and anti-racist practice is fundamental to this. We've set up an anti-racist thinking space for all staff to bring dilemmas and challenges they might face in practice and to help practitioners to develop their anti-racist practice.

Working with children and families

Leadership and organisational culture and values have a direct impact on practice and must visibly address inequalities caused by racism. In my local authority, our practice values are clearly defined and needed to be embedded within a practice model. We're now using the Signs of Safety practice framework to establish a strong foundation for our anti-racist work. Signs of Safety was developed and informed by lived experience of families, children and practitioners. Its roots are in developing a different way to work with families from indigenous backgrounds in Australia. The model positions families as the experts in their own lives and invites the practitioner to honour the family and the solutions they can bring to the challenges they face (Turnell and Murphy, 2017).

Reflecting on anti-racist leadership

Genuine anti-racist leadership requires personal and professional vulnerability. Leaders must be able to admit when they are unsure and to navigate complexity in a sensitive and thoughtful way. I often feel my words can be *'clunky'* but I'm committed to staying with the conversation and thinking and learning together with my team.

White leaders must be able to connect to the emotional experience of global majority colleagues. The reflective spaces where colleagues have shared their day-to-day lived experiences have been transformational in developing my thinking and I see naivety in my previous understanding of how racism and difference might be experienced in my organisation. A turning point for me was making the emotional connection to the pain and hurt in one of our reflective sessions when a black colleague said:

> *I was called a monkey when I was growing up and I don't want that for my children. I'm tired of it all. When we look for places to go on holiday, we try and find the countries that we think will be the least racist.*

More stories about the pain and injustice of racism have been shared within our leadership group and I'm grateful for colleagues' openness. Our conversations have led to deeper understanding of what it can mean to be an anti-racist ally and white colleagues are learning to step up, making anti-racist practice central to our thinking. Recently, a white manager stepped in to challenge a partner agency where a black social worker had identified racist decision making. In this instance, stepping into the role of white ally meant driving the challenge against racist practice and not leaving this to black colleagues. Global majority colleagues have had an opportunity to explore and articulate what might support them better as we develop our anti-racist practice. What is evident is that the journey to becoming an actively anti-racist organisation is something that we work towards together, keeping in mind our own position in relation to the Social Graces and what power and privilege we have been afforded.

Visibility is an essential element of anti-racist leadership. Leaders must respond to incidents or situations in a proactive way that demonstrates allyship and support. For example, when the case of Child Q (CHSCP, 2022) was in the press, we took an actively anti-racist stance in our communications to the workforce and were clear in our commitment to zero tolerance of racist behaviour in any shape or form. We also took steps to acknowledge and recognise the shock felt throughout the system at the treatment of this child. Silence is not acceptable.

The future

My organisation and leadership team are committed to anti-racism. There's much to do and we're realistic about immediate aims, but we are determined to become an organisation where anti-racist practice is core to our functioning. Leaders and staff across the service area are engaged and motivated to be involved in this work.

In our most recent staff health check, 66 per cent of staff said they felt children's social care to be an anti-racist and anti-discriminatory department which promotes inclusivity for all the organisation. Feedback suggested widespread awareness of the Anti-Racist Network Group and a strong desire for this work to continue. Staff also said they would like anti-racist approaches to be more strongly embedded in our practice approach so that our direct work with families is grounded on understanding experiences of racism and discrimination.

Conclusion

Our work in tackling racism and becoming an anti-racist organisation is in early formation but we've reasons to be optimistic about what we can achieve. We've made space and time to focus on the relationships between ourselves as leaders and across the wider staff group and this will impact relational understanding in our practice with children and families. It will also support us in our will to be a learning organisation that values and cares for the workforce and the community we serve.

At times, the task can feel overwhelming, but as leaders it's our responsibility to make our objectives tangible and manageable, keeping in mind the saying, *'When eating an elephant take one bite at a time'*.

Reflections

- Which of the Social Graces do you connect with and why?
- What does your organisation need to do to develop anti-racist practice?
- What would your next step be to develop anti-racist practice in your organisation?

References

Barnard, C (2021) *Intersectionality for Social Workers: A Practical Introduction to Theory and Practice.* London: Routledge.

Burnham, J (2012) Developments in Social GRRRAAACCEEESSS: Visible-Invisible and Voiced-Unvoiced. In Krause, I B (ed) *Mutual Perspectives: Culture and Reflexivity in Systemic Psychotherapy.* London: Karnac.

Campbell-Stevens, R (2020) Global Majority: We Need to Talk About Labels such as 'BAME'. [online] Available at: www.linkedin.com/pulse/global-majority-we-need-talk-labels-bame-campbell-stephens-mbe (accessed 8 November 2022).

CHSCP (2022) Local Child Safeguarding Practice Review : Child Q. City of Hackney Safeguarding Children's Partnership. [online] Available at: https://chscp.org.uk/wp-content/uploads/2022/03/Child-Q-PUBLISHED-14-March-22.pdf (accessed 21 November 2022).

Menzies Lyth, I (1959) The Functioning of Social Systems as a Defence Against Anxiety. In Menzies Lyth, I, *Containing Anxiety in Institutions. Selected Essays Vol 1.* London: Free Association Books.

Turnell, A and Murphy, T (2017) *Signs of Safety Comprehensive Briefing Paper.* 4th edition. Perth: Resolutions Consultancy. [online] Available at: www.signsofsafety.net/knowledgebank/ (accessed 8 November 2022).

Ziregbe, M (2022) Developing Anti-Racist Practice in Social Work Leadership. Research in Practice. [online] Available at: www.researchinpractice.org.uk/children/news-views/2022/may/developing-anti-racist-practice-and-promoting-diversity-in-social-work-leadership/ (accessed 8 November 2022).

CHAPTER 11

UNDERSTANDING RACIAL DYNAMICS IN SUPERVISION

Godfred Boahen

To Lana and Tamalia and hoping that you grow up in a more just world.

Introduction

This chapter advocates for 'race' to be made 'visible' in supervision. It explains why racial dynamics, while ever-present, are yet invisible, but can show in different behaviours by both supervisors and supervisees. A core principle of social work is that prevailing social structures result in different forms of bigotry including gender, sexuality, religion, 'race' and disability. From this vantage point, racism and other forms of oppression exist. Therefore, taking as a point of departure the *lived reality* of racism, I will examine how supervision can be used as a safe space to identify its manifestation in social care.

Overt discrimination is a hate crime in England and a contravention of professional standards and codes of ethics and conduct. Given this, racism in social care (including social work) is likely to be covert, so must be identified and addressed; I explore how this can be achieved. In so doing, I use the term '*Black*' to represent people of colour and '*White*' for the majority group in England – I acknowledge that these terms are contentious; however, they are commonly used for political and simplification purposes in the policy debates.

Policy and practice contexts

Notwithstanding social work's historical commitment to anti-racism, until recently there had been little examination of how racial oppression manifested in practice. Questions such as these were rarely addressed in the literature: how does racism unfold in the unique context of practice? What forms of racism do Black practitioners experience from people who use services and within the workplace? To what extent do social workers hold racist views and what mechanisms do they use to victimise others?

Arguably, there is an ongoing sector-led refocusing of the debates in social care, which is traceable to the murder of George Floyd, which itself led to the reinvigoration of anti-racist activism globally. There is now a profound change in the tone of the discussion – in the face of the established research evidence, the current interest in racism in social care is premised on a consensus that it exists. For instance, survey research commissioned by the Anti-Racist Steering Group, which includes sector leaders such as the Principal Social Workers' Network for Adults and Children and Families, Social Work England and What Works for Children's Social Care, found that 28 per cent of Black respondents reported experiencing racism from managers and colleagues at least once. Furthermore, it was found that 37 per cent of Black respondents had been victims of racism by service users and their families, while '*31% reported witnessing racism directed towards service users / families from colleagues and managers one or more times*' (Gurau and Bacchoo, 2021, p 9).

In policy terms, racial inequality in social care has become linked to strategies to support the post-Covid recovery of the workforce. For instance, in two inquiries, the Health and Social Care Select Committee noted that Black staff in health and care were more likely to experience bullying and harassment than their White colleagues, causing them greater rates of stress and mental illness (House of Commons, 2020). Building on this work and acknowledging the prevalence of racial inequality in social care, the Department of Health and Social Care (DHSC) launched the *Social Care Workplace Race Equality Standards* (SCWRES) in 2020. The SCWRES is a policy intervention to '*measure*' racial in/equality. Phase 1 completed in 2022 and the government stated commitment to national implementation, arguing that *local authorities will use [the SCWRES] data to create plans for ensuring staff from ethnic minority backgrounds are treated equally, feel included and valued, their health and wellbeing are prioritised, and they have access to culturally appropriate support.*

(DHSC, 2022)

This research and policy interest in racial (in)equality in the social care workplace throws the spotlight on supervision. While the literature suggests that supervision should support well-being, promote anti-oppressive practice, and enhance career development, in practice, managerialist and performance management models dominate (O'Donoghue and Engelbrecht, 2021). Consequently, the full anti-racist potential of supervision is not realised among Black social care professionals. Furthermore, because most managers are White, without careful critical reflection and organisational systems to prevent discrimination, supervision can be another site for (re)producing racial inequality and (re)traumatisation.

For these reasons, there is a need for an explicit commitment to anti-racist practice in supervision.

Picking up these themes, in the next sections I discuss why and how 'race' is ever-present in supervision, even where both supervisor and supervisee identify as White. I start by explaining 'race', a debunked concept which nevertheless shapes social and professional relationships. I argue that beliefs in 'race' can result in racism – often experienced by Black social workers – and I show that this manifests in microaggression, stress and trauma. I conclude with a practical advice for anti-racist supervision.

'Race' and power relations in supervision

In social care, supervision occurs in different contexts and several models can be used depending on the objectives of the supervisor. Peer-to-peer types are used by practitioners to achieve self-directed learning (Wilkins and Boahen, 2013) through, for example, action-learning sets (see Boahen et al, 2021). However, in contemporary times, supervision has taken a managerialist turn and it is likely to occur in a relationship dyad with a manager (supervisor) and supervisee. The former seeks a task-oriented approach to '*cases*' and to line manage the latter to ensure accountability and generate new learning to enhance performance (O'Donoghue and Engelbrecht, 2021). While the research shows that supervisees want supervision to be used as a space to address their emotional needs and support their well-being, this occurs infrequently (Newcomb, 2022).

This supervision dyad, or the one-to-one model, requires examination because its inherent power differences have implications for anti-racist practice. It is conceptualised as

> *an interpersonal transaction [in which] there is* the use of authority (the organisational/administrative *function), and exchange of information and ideas (the professional/educational function), and the expression of feelings (the emotional/ supportive function).*
>
> (Tsui, 2021, p 315, emphasis added)

The supervisor is more powerful because of their status in the organisation's hierarchy. As a 'manager' or 'supervisor' they have authority and power conferred on them by the agency to set tasks for the supervisee and they even determine the scheduling and agenda of supervision and model used. Their organisational status entitles them to give case direction and set timelines which the supervisee is obliged to follow. The supervisor also has power to determine career progression through performance management appraisals. Furthermore, the supervisor can even determine whether the discussions in the supervision call into question the supervisee's Fitness to Practice and refer them to the regulator for an investigation (Social Work England, 2021).

The inherent power differences between the supervisor and supervisee are more heightened if they are each from a different '*race*'. Where the supervisee is White, their racial status confers on them power and they can draw on this consciously or inadvertently, to question and challenge the authority of the Black supervisor. Where the supervisor or supervisee are White, '*race*' can be silenced to the extent that they will not question or challenge their respective racist assumptions or the racism experienced by a service user. Societal beliefs in existence of different '*races*' shape the lived experiences of supervisors and supervisees, whether they are conscious or not of this phenomenon. Therefore, in the next section, I examine manifestations of power relations stemming from beliefs in 'race' – racism, micro-aggression and stress and racial trauma – and how they become actualised in supervision.

'Race', racism and behaviours in supervision

In everyday language, 'race' is the belief that people's observable traits, for example skin and eye colour, height, size, etc – exemplify genetic differences which shape them physically, psychologically, emotionally and culturally. Although modern science has debunked this, the entrenched belief in separate 'races' persists and continues to influence societal and inter-personal relationships. We are socialised to believe that White and Black people are biologically distinct, and we believe we *know* this because we can *see* it through their different skin colours. Furthermore, historically, power relations in England and the global West are linked to this worldview and, consequently, we observe that White people are more likely to hold and exercise power within social care organisations.

Social work practice, including supervision, exists within systems and structures based on this misconception about racial differences. Furthermore, supervision occurs in contexts in which a White person is likely to be the supervisor and a Black person the supervisee, with the former exercising more power than the latter. However, in some cases, the supervisee may be White and the supervisor Black or both parties may identify as the same 'race'. Each of these racial dyads has important implications for how power relations manifest within that supervision interaction – some probable behaviours and their impacts are captured in the table below.

Table 11.1 Some probable behaviours and their impacts

Nature of the racial dyad	Possible behaviours	Impact
White supervisor and Black supervisee	• Supervisor feels uncomfortable discussing 'race' and racism about 'cases'	• Supervisee may feel shame and disgust about themselves because racism is not acknowledged

→

Table 11.1 (continued)

Nature of the racial dyad	Possible behaviours	Impact
	• Supervisor ignores the impact of their power in the supervision dynamic • Supervisee feels unable to discuss being racially victimised • Supervisee seeks to challenge supervisor's overt or covert racism • Supervisee remains silent about their experiences of racism	• Supervisee feels unsupported and (re) traumatised • Supervisee feels stressed and fearful • Supervisor feels deskilled or guilty for their actions • Racial oppression (in organisation and society) is reaffirmed and maintained • Supervisor may assert *whiteness* and power if challenged to take action about racism
White supervisor and White supervisee	• '*Race*' invisible – not discussed in supervision or it is dismissed as a possibility • Racist behaviour by supervisor and/ or supervisee unchallenged by either party	• Racial oppression is maintained • Deskilling of both professionals • Lack of critical reflection • Both parties can feel shame for not challenging the other's racist viewpoints • Both parties acknowledge their lack of knowledge or their racist assumptions and engage in mutual reflection and learning
Black supervisor and Black supervisee	• '*Race*' and racism acknowledged but both feel powerless to change anything, given the organisational and societal contexts	• Apathy • Moral injury – this is caused when people engage in actions that are against their ethical principles (Norman and Maguen, nd)

Table 11.1 (continued)

Nature of the racial dyad	Possible behaviours	Impact
	• Both use opportunity for critical reflection and mutual support	• Lack of commitment • Avoidance • Displaying powerlessness and helplessness; or • Engage in anti-racist activism in the workplace
Black supervisor and White supervisee	• Supervisor seeks to discuss race and racism in cases, to make them 'visible' • Supervisee challenges supervisor's authority • Supervisee asserts whiteness • Supervisor feels powerless – avoidance or seeks to assert authority • Supervisee takes this as opportunity to learn and understand racism	• Strained relationship • Supervisor is fearful of supervisee • Potential racist behaviours unchallenged • Moral injury • Productive self-reflection

Racism and supervision

These power relations inherent in perceived racial differences can also result in *racism*:

> The belief that humans may be divided into separate and exclusive bio-logical entities called 'races'; that there is a causal link between inherited physical traits and traits of personality, intellect, morality, and other cultural and behavioural features; and that some races are innately superior to others. The term is also applied to political, economic, or

legal institutions and systems that engage in or perpetuate discrimin-
ation on the basis of race or otherwise reinforce racial inequalities in
wealth and income, education, health [and social] care, civil rights,
and other areas.

(Smedley, 2021, emphasis added)

The definition above highlights two important dimensions of racial oppression relevant to the supervision dyad. Firstly, the belief in racial superiority can lead to preferential treatment for the majority group and, conversely, it fosters the exclusion of minority groups from services. From the organisational perspective, the majority group is likely to be favoured for leadership roles, including the provision of supervision. Since racism is a belief system, it influences inter-racial relationships even for people who may not see themselves as *'racist'*.

Supervisors and supervisees must be alive to how racism shapes their professional relationships. For instance, a White supervisor might consciously and deliberately decide to evaluate their Black supervisee's work poorly or doubt their account of events or *'challenge'* them when they report being victims of racism. Another possibility is that racism might be embedded in organisational processes and practice situations in such a way that its impact is difficult to *'prove'* or identify. The implication of this is that both the supervisor and supervisee will likely encounter victims of racial discrimination in their practice, and Black social workers will directly experience racial prejudice. Anti-racist practice in supervision requires them to take active steps to make *'race'* visible and ensure that they address it.

Micro-aggression in the supervision context

In social work, racism can also manifest as *micro-aggression*s, which are subtle forms of insults that Black people experience because of societal negative stereotypes about people of colour. Sometimes perpetrators of micro-aggression are unaware of their behaviours because they have been socialised in a way that normalises the demeaning of Black people. However, micro-aggression can be perpetrated deliberately because people are in powerful positions, thus enabling them to exercise their racist beliefs.

Otuyelu et al (2016) suggest that this form of racism (micro-aggression) falls into three types:

- **Micro-assaults:** these are conscious and deliberate displays of racism, such as using racial slurs and insults. In England, this overt racism is a hate crime which must be reported to the police.

- **Micro-insults:** verbal and non-verbal insults that are intended to disparage people's ethnicity and their culture. This can take the form of playful portrayal of someone's heritage, sometimes termed 'banter'; however, the intention is to demean and stereotype people.

- **Micro-invalidations:** These are '[c]ommunications that subtly exclude, negate or nullify the thoughts, feelings or experiential reality of a person of color' (DeAngelis, 2009). Black social workers may encounter this form of racism when in discussing their experiences of racism, White colleagues appear uncomfortable and they will ask for an equal emphasis on class discrimination or classism. This desire to change the conversation about racism can lead a Black social worker to feel that their lived-experience of racism has been invalidated or unrecognised. Similarly, social workers can also experience this in supervision when supervisors offer 'healthy challenge' to their report of being victims of racism, asking for 'categorical evidence that the person was racist'.

Our discussion on micro-aggression signifies that it can be covert and overt in social care/social work. For instance, people who use services may show hostility towards Black social workers. This can include telling them 'I do not want a Black social worker' or by making allegations against them or questioning their competence and capabilities because of their 'race'. However, in most cases, the racism is likely to be covert, as the research shows. Examples include:

- higher rates of bullying and harassment of Black social care professionals;

- questioning of Black social workers' character and challenging their 'attitude' to practice;

- referencing Black social workers as 'aggressive' or 'passive' or 'unwilling to put in the hours' or 'go the extra mile';

- Black social workers are more likely to be subject to Fitness to Practice investigations;

- families showing more resistance to Black social workers.

The key issue is that, whether covert or overt, the experience of racism can cause stress and trauma in victims, and this is explored further in the next section.

Examining racial trauma within the supervision context

The concepts *stress* and *trauma* explain the psychological, physiological and sometimes physical impact of racism on victims. Stress refers to our responses to perceived or actual risks to our well-being that arise in our environment. Regarding racism,

> *[even] the mere threat of [racial] prejudice is sufficient to elicit a physiological response, even in the absence of actual behavioral cues and before individuals have actually entered into the situation in which discrimination may potentially take place.*
>
> (Sawyer et al, 2012, p 1024)

While stress caused by racism adversely impacts on well-being, it is considered people have the internal resources to cope with the actual or perceived harm.

However, others can become overwhelmed by the impact of racism; they may find this overpowering to the extent that they are unable to cope psychologically, emotionally and sometimes physically (Kirkinis et al, 2021). Therefore, whether an incident of racial discrimination causes trauma or stress is relative to each person's internal coping mechanism. This means two Black supervisees who are victims of racism may show different symptoms of the harm caused to them – one could experience it as stress and the other as trauma. Witnessing even a new '*minor*' racial discrimination may become retriggering and remind a Black social worker of their previous encounters with racism. Furthermore, a new racist incident could be a compounding factor for some who have experienced several stresses, thereby having a cumulative effect, which can then become overwhelming.

Notwithstanding the relative and subjective impact of racial trauma and stress, they will affect supervisees' performances and their interaction with fellow professionals and people who use services. For instance, Black social workers can show signs of psychological distress such as anger and hyper-vigilance. They may also seek to avoid the families or professionals who are victimising them and this will come across as *non-engagement* (conversely non-engagement may occur with White social workers who show racist behaviours towards Black families). At the end of the scale of impact, victims may experience post-traumatic stress disorder which can manifest as sleeplessness, depression and other mental illness (Comas-Díaz et al, 2019).

This discussion implies this central message – *'race'* and racism should be discussed in supervision irrespective of the *'race'* of both parties, and especially where the two parties identify as different *'races'*. The next section, the conclusion, continues the theme of how supervision can be a form of anti-racist practice.

Conclusion: towards anti-racist practice in supervision

This chapter has sought to make *'race'* visible by showing how racial dynamics shape behaviours of supervisees and supervisors. The central thesis is that *'race'* is ever-present and confers power on those who identify as White, a situation that is amplified by organisational practices which mean that supervisors are also likely to be line managers. There is a pressing need for anti-racism in supervision. Anti-racist practice in this context of supervision has a tripartite meaning. It refers to the process and methods which supervisors and supervisees deliberately and actively employ to uncover how *'race'* and racism have shaped conduct and decision making in practice. Secondly, it is about rejecting any form of racism on ethical and moral grounds and in an anti-oppressive manner, drawing on the law, theory and practice to work against it. Finally, anti-racist practice refers to how supervisors and social care organisations ensure that Black supervisees can discuss the racism they have experienced and the support they need to address it. To achieve this, supervisors who identify as White need to understand that their racial identity and positions in organisations confer power on them. The Critical Conversation model (Chandra, 2020) is an open-access resource that explains steps that supervisors can take to understand how their own power affects the supervisory relationship. It also calls for critical reflection and an open self-dialogue about the power that accrues from being part of the dominant White group. Supervisors also need to commit to a different model of supervision that, henceforth, will address *'race'* and racism. This should be done in partnership with supervisees. In practice, it means the avoidance of sole use of managerialist approaches, which focus predominantly on discussing '*cases*'. Supervision should include '*clinical*' and anti-oppressive elements which recognise that our socio-political context can generate behaviours based on racist assumptions and that these can adversely affect the well-being of Black social workers. This new model of supervision should be developed with the Black supervisee by asking them what actions the supervisor (and organisation) must take to make supervision a safe space for them.

Reflections

For supervisors

- Use the Critical Conversations model (Chandra, 2020) – what does it teach you about your power as a supervisor?

- Identify your '*race*' – what is your racial identity? How does your '*race*' enable you to exercise power in your workplace? Who are you able to exercise power over and what is their '*race*'?

- What can you do to exercise your power ethically?

For supervisees

- Identify your '*race*' – what is your racial identity? Does it make you more powerful or powerless relative to other people from a different '*race*'? If so, why and how?

- Research your organisation that you work in – what support exists for people of different '*races*' who experience racism?

References

Boahen, G et al (2021) Developing Reflective Models of Supervision: The Role of the United Kingdom Professional Association. In O'Donoghue, K and Engelbrecht, L (eds) *The Routledge International Handbook of Social Work Supervision* (pp 3–12). Abingdon: Routledge.

Chandra, C (2020) *Critical Conversations in Social Work Supervision*. [online] Available at: https://practice-supervisors.rip.org.uk/wp-content/uploads/2021/01/PT_Critical-conversations-in-social-work-supervision_Final.pdf (accessed 2 November 2022).

Comas-Díaz, L, Hall, G N and Neville, H A (2019) Racial Trauma: Theory, Research, and Healing: Introduction to the Special Issue. *American Psychologist*, 74(1): 1–5.

DeAngelis, T (2009) Unmasking 'Racial Micro Aggressions'. American Psychological Association. [online] Available at: www.apa.org/monitor/2009/02/microaggression (accessed 2 November 2022).

Department for Health and Social Care (2022) *People at the Heart of Care: Adult Social Care Reform*. [online] Available at: www.gov.uk/government/publications/people-at-the-heart-of-care-adult-social-care-reform-white-paper/people-at-the-heart-of-care-adult-social-care-reform (accessed 2 November 2022).

Gurau, O and Bacchoo, A (2021) Anti-racism Report. *What Works for Children's Social Care*. [online] Available at: https://whatworks-csc.org.uk/wp-content/uploads/WWCSC_SWE_PSWN_Anti-Racism_Full_Report_March2022.pdf (accessed 2 November 2022).

House of Commons Health and Social Care Select Committee (2020) *Delivering Core NHS and Care Services during the Pandemic and Beyond*. [online] Available at: https://committees.parliament.uk/publications/2793/documents/27577/default/ (accessed 2 November 2022).

Kirkinis, K, Pieterse, A L, Martin, C, Agiliga, A and Brownell, A (2021) Racism, Racial Discrimination, and Trauma: A Systematic Review of the Social Science Literature. *Ethnicity & Health*, 26(3): 392–412.

Newcomb, M (2022) Supportive Social Work Supervision as an Act of Care: A Conceptual Model. *British Journal of Social Work*, 52(2): 1070–88.

Norman, S B and Maguen, S (nd) *Moral Injury*. [online] Available at: www.ptsd.va.gov/professional/treat/cooccurring/moral_injury.asp#.Y7iCtTDKXzQ.link (accessed 2 November 2022).

O'Donoghue, K and Engelbrecht, L (2021) Introduction: Supervision in Social Work. In O'Donoghue, K and Engelbrecht, L (eds) *The Routledge International Handbook of Social Work Supervision*. Abingdon: Routledge.

Otuyelu, F, Graham, W and Kennedy, S A (2016) The Death of Black Males: The Unmasking of Cultural Competence and Oppressive Practices in a Micro-Aggressive Environment. *Journal of Human Behavior in the Social Environment*, 26(3–4): 430–6.

Sawyer, P J et al (2012) Discrimination and the Stress Response: Psychological and Physiological Consequences of Anticipating Prejudice in Interethnic Interactions. *American Journal of Public Health*, 102(5): 1020–6.

Smedley, A (2021) Racism. *Encyclopedia Britannica.* [online] Available at: www.britannica.com/topic/racism (accessed 2 November 2022).

Social Work England (2021) Raise a Concern about a Social Worker. [online] Available at: www.socialworkengland.org.uk/concerns/raise-a-concern/ (accessed 2 November 2022).

Tsui, M (2021) The Comprehensive Model of Social Work Supervision. In O'Donoghue, K and Engelbrecht, L (eds) *The Routledge International Handbook of Social Work Supervision* (pp 309–20). Abingdon: Routledge.

Wilkins, D and Boahen, G (2013) *Critical Analysis Skills for Social Workers.* Maidenhead: Open University Press.

CHAPTER 12

SOCIAL WORKER'S RELATIONSHIP WITH CPD

Tanya Moore

Introduction

Social workers love CPD. Good learning develops thinking, confidence and morale and creates much needed space to think about practice.

We relish that feeling of our thinking being stretched and the adrenaline rush that comes when we connect new understanding and theory to our own experience and realise there's more than we originally saw to a situation.

We all have our own relationship with learning, but we know learning can create vulnerability as it moves us away from the familiar and challenges existing beliefs. New knowledge can inform and develop our thinking for the future, but it can also cause us to critically review decisions we've made in the past. When we dare to question our past decisions in the light of new knowledge, this can be a difficult and uncomfortable experience. However, there's always more to know and in the complex world of social work, where we often work with subjectivity and judgement rather than definitive truth, our desire to continually develop our ability to think in an informed and critical way by taking on new knowledge, understandings and perspective is non-negotiable.

My chapter is about the social worker's relationship with CPD and how we can make the most out of it. Employers of social workers have a responsibility to provide good CPD opportunities but, ultimately, we must also take responsibility for our professional development by taking an active role in directing the CPD on offer and in seeking out and investing in our own opportunities to develop our professional interests and practice. We all have our own personal response to the challenge of professional development, and while some of this may be about the type of learning on offer, much of it is about our original experiences of learning and how these have set us up to think about learning as adults.

The nature of CPD

Social work CPD can broadly be divided into

(i) statutory knowledge and functions;

(ii) theory and skills development.

The statutory stuff is the bare bones of UK practice. This is the law and its associated guidance and interpretation as well as the processes each department will have in place for enacting its legal responsibilities. We need to have good understanding of the powers and duties that underpin social work if we are to practice lawfully and meet our statutory duties. We also need to be familiar with the processes our own employers have put in place to implement their responsibilities. If the law is a framework for our practice, the theory that informs thinking and the skills that enhance ability to connect usefully with people are the fabric. It's the way social workers see the world and the approaches we use to address difficulty that differentiate us from other professionals who work to the same legal framework. Both are essential for safe and effective social work practice, but the reality is that cash-strapped employers are more likely to focus on the concrete statutory knowledge and, for many of us, the CPD offered by our employers doesn't reflect the breadth of learning we feel we should be doing.

In 2018, as part of my own professional development, I completed a questionnaire study of the CPD experiences of 68 social workers in England. I found that, for the respondents to my study, 42 per cent of CPD undertaken was on the knowledge required for statutory functions (ie safeguarding and application of the Mental Health Act and Mental Capacity Act), 24 per cent was on specific subject knowledge, assessment and practice models and 16 per cent was on leadership or education (eg Practice Educator or ASYE Assessor). Yet Reflective Supervision, which is core to social work practice, was the subject of only 2 per cent of CPD and Human Rights, or the value base of social work, was 1 per cent.

If we mostly look to our employers to provide CPD opportunities, my findings won't be surprising. Local authority employers are required to provide dedicated time, resources and opportunities for social workers to plan, reflect and think creatively about their CPD. This is laid out in The Standards for Employers of Social Workers in England (LGA, 2020) and should be seen as a blueprint for all other social worker employers. But the reality is that while local authorities have such tight budgets, their priority is likely to be ensuring their statutory duties are upheld so reliance upon our employers for CPD might be at cost of the broader intellectual refreshment we seek for practice. Social work is so much more than a statutory duty and our sources of knowledge are much wider.

Of course, CPD is requisite for professional registration. At the time of writing, we're required to annually submit written reflections on two experiences of CPD to Social Work England, the registering body for social workers. Finding CPD to record isn't a problem; my study found a yearly average of five CPD experiences each (Moore, 2020). This was just the formal stuff such as courses and conferences. Social Work England also acknowledges all the other wonderful informal learning: the book we read (perhaps this one!), the webinar we attended, the rich team meeting discussion we led. If we're developing our professional practice, it's CPD. And if we can demonstrate this through written reflections, SWE will accept it as such. The point about continuing professional development is just that; it's continual. We do it all the time.

However, social workers are hugely pushed for time. We all know that when we take a day to attend a course, our work stacks up and we have to somehow catch up. Balancing our need to develop with our need to stay on top of our work is an ongoing tension. Social workers manage this to different degrees through a combination of prioritising, time management and willingness to invest our own time into CPD. The difficulties faced by social workers in taking on CPD are well understood. Time, back-cover at work, money for fees and books and availability of childcare or support with other caring responsibilities is always scarce. For Black social workers, there's the additional risk of being marginalised by being the only or one of a small group of Black people on the course.

My study found that although social workers do regularly cancel training courses because of work pressures, the interest and support of our managers and colleagues has a significant impact on how effectively we can engage with our CPD opportunities. With good support, a little bit of CPD can go a long way. So, by creating a work culture in which learning is cherished and nourished, we can help each other to continually develop professionally.

Creating a culture of professional development

There are lots of ways to do this, from remembering to check in with a colleague about how their course is going, to building time into team meetings or running workshops in which learning can be shared. My study highlighted the importance of team managers in encouraging CPD. This of course includes practical support but also interest and encouragement. It's great practice for both supervisor and supervisee to make time in each supervision to talk about current professional development. This might include a conversation about courses but it's just as likely to be new thinking that arose from an encounter with a family or another professional. It might be a video or a podcast that has sparked a new and helpful perspective that will influence practice. For managers wishing to encourage development in their team, it's helpful to know that applicability to practice supports engagement with CPD so taking proactive steps to build newly acquired knowledge into the team's practice doubles up as team development as well as creative and effective encouragement of individual team member's development.

Just as it's not enough for social workers to rely wholly on their employers for CPD, it's not good for employers to restrict their offer to statutory fact top-ups. Social workers need time and space to develop their thinking, and it follows that an organisation that supports time to think will be an organisation of sophisticated and well-developed thinkers! Beddoe (2009) writes about learning organisations who prescribe the learning required of their staff, thus restricting the development of knowledge; if we only learn what the organisation tells us we need to know, she says, there's no scope for new thought to be brought into an organisation. So an organisation teaches its staff how to *do*, not how to *think*; it develops the knowledge base and not the potential. This might be understood to be an unconsciously defensive move by an organisation that is itself under siege of increasing expectation and decreasing resource, but it's obviously restrictive for the organisation as well as the worker as the creative potential of its professional workforce is stifled by a reluctance to explore the unknown.

For critical pedagogue Freire (1972), education can't be neutral; when we make decisions about curriculum, teaching methods and policies, we're expressing ideological choice. Co-producing social work education and training with students and with people who draw upon social care services is an example of liberationist pedagogy in action, but if we rely solely upon our local government employers and regulator for our CPD, might we invite the reverse? Allowing politically driven and external organisations to control our professional development costs us our ability to be independent thinkers and risks our position as agitators and challengers. Employers have a responsibility to social work development, but social workers have a responsibility to social work development, too.

Complete and delete

It's also important to think about how the learning required for CPD takes place. If we attend a course in which learning is *'delivered'* (I shudder whenever I hear such transactional terminology applied to either social care or education!), perhaps through a lecture or simplistic e-learning course, there's a risk that the information offered will effectively hover for a little while and then float away. It's not unusual for learners to forget everything they were told on a course within a day or even an hour! Anyone who has completed one of those mandatory e-learning courses where we're required to hold a series of facts just long enough to answer the quiz at the end may know exactly what I mean.

It was the influential pedagogue Dewey (1897) who first said that learners' heads can't be simply filled with knowledge; learners create their own knowledge by relating what happens in the classroom to their real world experiences. This *'constructivist'* approach to learning heavily influences social work education in which learning and experience are synthesised to create the conditions for developing knowledge and understanding. Good teachers are facilitators; they guide as learners experience and interact with their environments. So whether it's the traditional *'talk and chalk'* or the more contemporary *'complete and delete'* approach to training, a presentation of facts on its own can be limited in its effectiveness. As learners, we need space to engage with the presented information and make sense of it by connecting it to our own experience.

To stay with learning theory (pedagogy) for a little longer, it's *'social constructivist'* educators who recognise the role of social and cultural influence in the development of knowledge. This brings me back to our role as team members, colleagues and friends in supporting, sharing and encouraging professional development. Across our professional social work community, *'communities of practice'* are formed in teams, study groups and wider professional groups such as subject specific interest groups, membership organisations or across social media groups and platforms. Beginners join at the periphery of their community but, in time, move to the centre as experienced *'old timers'* (Lave and Wenger, 1991). Learning happens through the development of relationships within the community. For social workers, this can be seen as our journey through student placements and subsequent post-qualifying career as we become more established within our professional community. Often, the original relationship with our practice educator has lasting impact on social workers throughout our careers, but the interest in our development that's shown by our peers, supervisors and managers also has a significant impact on the success or otherwise of our ongoing learning.

Relational

Perhaps it's no surprise that the development for professionals specialising in relational approaches to practice should be so heavily influenced by relationships. My own research into the emotional experience of CPD (Moore, 2020) takes this a stage further to suggest that our individual approach to CPD is influenced by our earliest experiences of learning. So if we were lucky enough to enjoy positive learning experiences in our formative years, perhaps we were allowed to understand that it's OK to make mistakes, that learning can be fun and that we are worthy of encouragement, then there's a good chance we'll feel the same way about learning now. But if learning was a more difficult experience, perhaps because of an unrecognised learning difficulty or lack of support from the grown ups who mattered to us, then learning is likely to be a more troubling experience now.

I suggest there are powerful unconscious dynamics at play in the way we approach our CPD and that just as we need to consider unconscious emotional responses and exchanges in our practice, so it's true for our learning. Attending to the emotional experience of CPD for our supervisees, our colleagues, our students and ourselves may be just as important as attending to the practical.

Conclusion

Just like social work practice, social work CPD relies upon our values, commitment and personal resources to be effective. It also demands that our employers are willing to be courageous and creative in their offer and that they are guided by social worker's expertise when designing the training calendar. Employers also need to allow space and support for individual autonomy to be exercised as individual social workers also make their own decisions about how their practice might be developed.

There's a powerful relational element to CPD that also should not be overlooked. Our ability to develop professionally is significantly impacted by the response we receive from our managers and colleagues. It's for each of us to contribute to the creation of a thinking community in which professional development is supported and valued and new understanding is shared. It's also for each of us to develop understanding about how our own emotional responses impact our relationship with our CPD.

Reflections

- How can you help to create a supportive culture of professional development within your team?
- What sort of CPD opportunities do you usually create for yourself and/or your colleagues?
- How would you describe your response to learning opportunities?

References

Beddoe, L (2009) Creating Continuous Conversation: Social Workers and Learning Organizations. *Social Work Education*, 28(7): 722–36.

Dewey, J (1897) My Pedagogic Creed. *The School Journal*, 54(3): 77–80.

Freire, P (1972) Education: Domestication or Liberation? *Prospects*, 2(2): 173–81.

Lave, J and Wenger, E (1991) *Situated Learning: Legitimate Peripheral Participation*. Cambridge: Cambridge University Press.

LGA (2020) *The Standards for Employers of Social Workers in England 2020*. Local Government Association. [online] Available at: www.local.gov.uk/standards-employers-social-workers-england-2020 (accessed 8 November 2022).

Moore, T (2020) *The Emotional Experience of Continuing Professional Development for Social Workers*. PhD thesis, Tavistock and Portman NHS Foundation Trust/University of Essex.

CHAPTER 13

OUR WELL-BEING

Leire Agirre

Why well-being?

You may be wondering why I chose to write a chapter on well-being in a book about practice.

My interest was sparked many years ago, when I witnessed some colleagues and friends struggle in their social work careers. The first was a fellow social work student, who found the difficult nature of her studies and placements caused her distress and seemed to trigger previous mental health issues. The second was a friend who decided to study social work later in her career. Though she thrived through the academic studies, once qualified, she found the emotional and bureaucratic demands very difficult, and this caused her significant stress. After a few periods of sickness, she gave up her career in social work.

It seemed to me that neither of my friends received the support they needed at the beginning of their difficulties. Both said supervision wasn't a space where they could reflect on their emotional responses to their work and so they had both struggled. By the time they were off work with stress, it seemed like a point of no return. I recall them saying they felt like they were the only ones struggling, *people don't talk about their well-being, they don't say when emotions are difficult*. It left me thinking about what I or others could have done to notice and support them earlier on. It got me questioning whether they were the exception. I began to wonder what it was really like for social workers.

Understanding social workers' well-being

Issues about social workers' well-being are not new, and studies conducted in several countries have found high levels of stress and burnout (Grant and Kinman, 2012). A 2018 report on working conditions of UK social workers (Boichat and Ravalier, 2018) found that, compared to the UK national average, social workers were exposed to chronically poor working conditions, and these were influencing outcomes such as high levels of dissatisfaction in the role and high levels of both presenteeism and social workers intending to leave the profession. The report also demonstrated working conditions that were poorer than the UK national average. The exception was in the level of peer support received which was seen as much more positive. However, in comparison to 2017 figures, 2018 working conditions had consistently worsened. Levels of job dissatisfaction were high and turnover intentions, presenteeism and stress were consistent issues.

Around the time of this report, I had been appointed to a Principal Social Worker role and needed to know more about the experience of social workers in my own local authority. So, I added a well-being questionnaire to the annual Social Workers Health Check. My questionnaire identified several issues that were impacting social workers' well-being and it became obvious to me that, for practice to thrive, social workers' well-being needed to be understood and supported. My interest in workforce well-being was ignited and a period of collaboration with other professionals on the understanding of workforce well-being for social workers began.

The work was cast into sharp focus by Covid when the importance of well-being became apparent to us all. For many, homeworking during the pandemic challenged existing support structures, restricting opportunities to connect. A recent study (McFadden et al, 2021) on the quality of working life for health and social care workers during the pandemic found that participants were doing increased levels of overtime, services held extensive waiting lists and staff struggled under the increased administration and complexity of cases. The study reflects a struggling health and social care workforce with participants reconsidering their professional futures to protect their well-being. Out of all the professionals who felt overwhelmed by the increased pressures, social workers were reported to have felt the largest impact. The study also found that social workers' mental well-being and quality of working life had decreased more than most over the course of the Covid-19 pandemic and social workers' well-being was lower than almost all other professions (midwives' well-being was found to be even lower).

The 2021 Annual Membership survey by BASW (2022) found that social workers consider the impact we have on other's well-being to be highly rewarding; most of us are happy to be in the profession. But the survey also found struggles with administrative burdens, inadequate staffing and over-full workloads. More than a fifth of the 2062 social workers and students who responded said that working during the peak of Covid had negatively affected their mental health and continued to do so. The 2021 Social Worker's Healthcheck (LGA, 2021) report shows social workers have found it difficult to feel positive and to maintain well-being.

The average career of a social worker is just eight years (Curtis et al, 2010), so it's reasonable to ask what we can do to address social worker well-being and how effective this may be in increasing retention across our profession. We must consider how we equip social work students and professionals to navigate the emotional distress encountered on an almost daily basis, and I think a key element to consider is the development of emotional intelligence and self-awareness.

Social work stress

Social work stress can be caused by bureaucracy, administrative burdens, high caseloads, lack of autonomy, lack of reflective spaces and access to peer support. Importantly, it can be caused by lack of time and space to process the difficult emotions we encounter in our day-to-day practice.

Where we are stressed and struggling, our thoughts can become clouded, and we are much less of an effective conduit for change. Grant and Kinman's (2012) work with students included piloting 'Well-being Days' in which stress management skills such as relaxation, time management, mindfulness, peer coaching and social support were explored. Students who attended found the sessions to be informative and helpful and there's an argument for employers to offer similar sessions for social workers.

Emotional intelligence

Emotional intelligence is the capacity of a person to recognise their own emotions and those of others. It provides adaptability in the face of change as well as confidence, self-motivation and the ability to regulate emotions. It's a key skill for social workers; research with social work students found they were better able to manage stress if they had good emotional intelligence (Grant and Kinman, 2012). Good emotional intelligence means we can identify and empathise with other people but, importantly, we can also see our own emotions as separate from the other person's. So we're less likely to become over-involved in a way that's confusing and unhelpful to others and detrimental to our own ability to think clearly and protect our well-being. The social work curriculum should address how emotional intelligence can be increased and social workers' CPD (continuing professional development) should highlight the importance of emotional intelligence as a core skill. This would better prepare and support us to differentiate our own emotions from those of people we support.

Social work is relational. Our practice is contained and supported by the relationships we form and the high value in which we hold others. I propose that we extend that regard to the relationship we have with ourselves, and we take steps to prioritise our own needs. Consideration of our own emotional responses develops self-awareness and our ability to discern external from internal struggles and to adapt our practice to varying situations. The same applies to awareness of our own well-being; a feeling of being well helps our clarity of mind, and allows us to apply our skills, knowledge and relational awareness.

Resilience through interaction

Although well-being can be supported, even the most resilient and emotionally intelligent social workers would find it difficult to thrive in poor working conditions. Resilience doesn't lie solely within the individual social worker; it's an interaction between the worker, the workplace, the culture and the physical environment. Employers must use the tools available to them to identify factors that impact well-being. But, as social workers, we must also engage with the tools on offer. For example, when we're asked to complete the annual Social Worker's Health Check mentioned above, it's important we take the time to complete this in a meaningful way that gives a clear picture of our experience. This helps Principal Social Workers understand the local social work environment and present a clear picture of how organisations can act to better support social workers in their day-to-day work.

Professional trust and autonomy

It's important that, as social workers, we get to experience a good level of autonomy in our practice. We are professionals, and where we are respected and trusted as such by our employers and managers, we're less likely to feel disempowered by the bureaucratic systems and processes within which we work. So those of us who manage others should ask ourselves whether there's anything we could change to increase autonomy within our teams. The very process of discussing the balance of good support with autonomy can be helpful for our well-being as it's empowering for all of us to be allowed our voice and to be an active part of the creation of solutions.

Supportive and reflective supervision is essential for resilience and can reduce the risk of burnout. Social workers are routinely involved in what can be difficult and distressing situations and the need to explore emotions while keeping a balanced perspective and judgement is well understood. But it's also helpful to look at success; *'What have I contributed?' 'What difference did I make to that person?'*. Being present to the impact of our practice, honing on our sense of accomplishment, can help bring the needed balance to the emotional demand and complexity of the work.

Practices to support well-being

For some of us, mindfulness and meditation practices can help develop our emotional intelligence, sense of self and well-being. Meditation reminds us our emotional state is impermanent and our thoughts and feelings can fleet and change. Our thoughts are the creation of our own minds and taking time to observe them as such can help us set worrying thoughts aside. Stress is often caused by thoughts of what may happen rather than what really happens. Meditation practices can free us to the realisation of the present moment in which thoughts and worries do not control our day-to-day but where we simply witness them as phenomena in our minds. This can in turn help calm the mind and provide peace and tranquillity.

There are many free online resources, such as mediation apps, that are easily available. Your local Buddhist centre might have free resources and Mindfulness Based Stress Reduction courses are widely available and often free or low in cost. Organisations such as Mind and NHS Well-being centres will also guide you to good local resources (addresses to links at the end of this chapter).

Some social work employers have now begun to recognise the benefit of well-being approaches at work and are beginning to offer courses such as managing worries, yoga, mindfulness and meditation. Some employers offer free weekly classes to their employees, and some have trained Well-being Champions to support and enhance healthy work environments. There are also Mental Health First Aiders, who can spot early signs of mental ill-health and signpost people to appropriate support. This is an important offer to social workers as it shows their employer understands the demands of the work and is committed to support social workers in their careers for the long term.

Strong networks of supportive relationships are a protective factor and can be a key aspect of self-care. Emotional support of colleagues is essential for the maintenance of a social worker's sense of well-being and purpose. Although disengagement from and even avoidance of our teams can be a common response to stress, it helps us to stay connected and participate in the team's life and activities. Social work managers can create connected spaces such as virtual and face-to-face meetings, coffee meet ups and even social events outside of work. Buddying people in teams can be a way to encourage supportive relationships and meeting up in the office can be particularly important for people living alone. Peer support in social work is core to the resilience of social workers and we should foster and nurture spaces where it's available. Other practices can support well-being. As a young social worker in a specialist mental health team, I used daily visualisation. When leaving the building, I would see my work staying in that space, and as the door closed it was all contained in the building until I opened the door again. You could try visualising your work staying in a room or going in a box, as you finish the day, and only opening up as you allow it to, when the day begins again.

Whatever your thing, go and do it!

I practice meditation daily and I know the many benefits it has brought me in my personal and professional life. I walk and do yoga daily and that works for me, but that may not chime with you. I know people who like Pilates and breath work, but you may prefer painting, crafting, dancing or running.

There's plenty of research saying that exercise of any kind brings huge benefits to physical and mental health. The key here is ... what works for you? What do you do now? Or even ... what would you love to do? Whatever your thing ... go and do it!

The trick is to identify what helps you maintain your well-being, then commit to it and include it as part of the daily habits needed for your life, and for sound robust and empathic social work practice. I see this as a professional requirement and consider it well worth a place in our busy social worker diaries!

Social work is about promoting the rights and well-being of others, but how we look out for ourselves has a direct impact on our ability to do this. When we consider the relational nature of our practice, let's not forget the relationship we have with ourselves!

Reflections

- How can I use supervision to talk about my well-being and/or that of the person I am supervising?
- What activities do I find useful to help differentiate work from the rest of my life?
- What activities could I introduce into work life and into personal life to support my well-being?

Footnote

A vision for social work, a call for reflection and action

Behind this chapter lies a lot more than words can express; a little book of notes or commitments that began almost five years ago. At that time, I gave my word to contribute to the creation of a well-being framework for social workers in the UK and beyond to cover the lifespan of a social worker.

My writing this chapter reaffirms my commitment to co-create a common vision, for a well-being framework to nurture social workers from the minute we choose to grow into a social worker to the time we move on from the profession. My invitation throughout this chapter is that you look internally and externally and reflect on how you may choose to contribute to your own well-being and then to a framework of well-being for social work.

(Loving Kindness or Meta meditation/mantra)

May I be at ease, joyful, supported & thrive

May all social workers be ease, joyful, supported & thrive

May all practitioners be at ease, joyful, supported & thrive

May all people be at ease, restored, supported & thrive.

A special thank you and acknowledgement to Juan Serrano, Ajahn Amaro, Jermaine Ravalier, Gerry Nosowska, Ruth Allen, Gail Kinman, Louise Grant, Neil Thompson, Tanya Moore, Sarah Range, Fran Leddra, Jilly Albony, Paola Koala, Mark Harvey and many others for sharing your knowledge and infectious passion at various times and events, as it has poured into every word and in contribution to *Our well-being.*

This chapter is dedicated with Love to Sue, may you be at ease, joyful and thriving.

Resources

Mind – www.Mind.org.uk

Oxford Mindfulness: Free online mindfulness sessions – www.oxfordmindfulness.org/free-online-mindfulness-course-sessions/

NHS England: Staff mental health and well-being hubs – www.england.nhs.uk/supporting-our-nhs-people/support-now/staff-mental-health-and-wellbeing-hubs/

BASW: Social Work Professional Support Service (PSS) – www.basw.co.uk/professional-support-service

Neil Thompson Academy: Free resources – https://neilthompson.info/free-resources-from-neil/

References

BASW (2022) *The BASW Annual Survey of Social Workers and Social Work 2021*. [online] Available at: www.basw.co.uk/system/files/resources/basw_annual_survey_summary_report_2021.pdf (accessed 8 November 2022).

Boichat, C and Ravalier, J (2018) *UK Social Workers: Working Conditions and Well-being*. [online] Available at: www.basw.co.uk/system/files/resources/Working%20Conditions%20%20Stress%20(2018)%20pdf.pdf (accessed 8 November 2022).

Curtis, L, Moriarty, J and Netten, A (2010) The Expected Working Life of a Social Worker. *British Journal of Social Work*, 40(5): 1628–43.

Grant, L and Kinman, G (2012) Enhancing Well-Being in Social Work Students: Building Resilience in the Next Generation. *Social Work Education*, 31(5): 605–21.

LGA (2021) *The Standards for Employers of Social Workers*. [online] Available at: https://local.gov.uk/publications/standards-employers-social-workers-national-report-summary-2021 (accessed 8 November 2022).

McFadden, P, Gillen, P, Moriarty, J, Mallett, J, Schroder, H, Ravalier, J, Currie, D, Nicholl, P, Neill, R and McGrory, S (2021) Health and Social Care Workers' Quality of Working Life and Coping while Working during the COVID-19 Pandemic: Phase 3 10th May 2021–2nd July 2021: Findings from a UK Survey. [online] Available at: https://pure.ulster.ac.uk/ws/files/100473155/Report_3_V8.pdf (accessed 21 November 2022).

Index

anonymity, online, 60–1
anti-racist activism, 116
anti-racist leadership, 103, 112
   and Anti-Racist Network Group,
      107, 109, 112
   commitment of, 109–10
   future of, 112
   and need for change, 105–7
   reflecting on, 110–11
   and Series of
      Conversations, 105–7
   surfacing of experiences and
      emotions, 107–9
   understanding difference,
      103–5
   and visibility, 111
   working with children and
      families, 110
Anti-Racist Network Group, 107,
   109, 112
Anti-Racist Steering Group, 116
Asset Based Community
   Development (ABCD), 37
asynchronous interactions, in online
   environment, 62
authority, in cyberspace, 62–3
autism, and discrimination, 76

being human, 80–1
benign disinhibition, of online
   activities, 60

Camerados, 47–9
Care Act 2014, 35, 48
care home, 79–80

change, need for, 105–7
Child Poverty Action Group
   (CPAG), 96, 97
Child Protection Plans, 97
Child Welfare Inequalities
   Project, 97
Children Act 1989, 98
Children's Services Department, 83
Community Food shops, 98
community strengths-based
   model, 37
community-based
   safeguarding, 51–2
connections
   impact of, 11–12
   keys to, 12–13
continuing professional
   development (CPD), 5, 135
   complete and delete, 133–4
   constructivist approach, 133–4
   culture of, 132–3
   and education and training, 133
   and emotional intelligence, 140
   nature of, 130–2
   overview, 129–30
   professional registration, 131
   relational, 134–5
   reliance on employers for, 131
   statutory knowledge and
      functions, 130
   theory and skills
      development, 130
   time management, 131–2
Covid-19 pandemic, 56, 67, 97

CPD. *See* continuing professional development (CPD)
Critical Conversation model, 125
cyberstalking, 58–60

digital assault, 58–60
digital professionalism, 56
disinhibition effect, of online activities, 60
dissociative anonymity, online identities, 60–1

eco-social work, 90
emotional connections, 12, 111
emotional intelligence, 140
empathetic connection, 1
empathy, 18, 26–7, 30
EMPOWER model, 26, 32
  empathy, 26–7, 30
  empowerment, 29, 31
  motivation, 27, 30
  observation, 28, 31
  purposeful person-centred approach, 27–8, 30
  restorative and reflective approach, 29–30, 31
  whole-system approach, 28, 31
environmental concerns, 84
environmental sustainability, 85, *see also* sustainability
e-professionalism, 55, 56, *see also* online relationships

factual writing, 17
Floyd, George, 105, 116
food banks, 98
food vouchers for holiday breaks, 98

free 15 hours childcare, 98
free school meals, 98

Global Definition of Social Work (IFSW), 90
green social work, 90

hate crime, 115
Healthy Start programme, 98
household support fund, 98
human rights, 4, 35, 49
  and poverty, 100
  and social work, 73

identity prism, online, 63–4
individual behaviour change, and sustainability, 86–7
inequalities, challenging, 76
intersectionality, 107
invisibility, in online environment, 61–2

Joseph Rowntree Foundation (JRF), 96
journey into social work, 73–4

language use, 46–7
learning disabilities, and discrimination, 76

majority group, 122
meditation, 142
memories, core, 8
Mental Health First Aiders, 142
micro-aggressions, and supervision, 122–4
micro-assaults, 123

micro-insults, 123
micro-invalidations, 123
Monroe, Jack, 99
motivation, 27, 30

names of people, inclusion in
    writing, 16
neighbour, and safeguarding, 49–51

observation, 28, 31
online practice, 68
    asynchronicity, 62
    authenticity, need for, 67
    changing intimacy and
        relationships, 66–7
    commodification of
        values, identities and
        relationships, 65–6
    compared with offline
        practice, 57
    digital assault, 58–60
    disinhibition effect, 60
    dissociative anonymity, 60–1
    identity prism, 63–4
    invisibility, 61–2
    narrative aspect, 64
    performance aspect, 64
    positive, 57–8
    relational aspect, 64–5
    risk and harm dimensions, 58
    status and authority
        minimisation, 62–3
ordinary activities, 80–1
    Enid's story, 78–9
    importance of, 71
    Ken's story, 78–9
    Maisie's story, 79–80
    Theo's story, 74–7

organisational structures, and
    racism, 108
overt discrimination, 115

peer reflection, 14
peer support, 142
personal and professional roles,
    distinction between, 67
personal contribution,
    importance of, 39
person-centred approach, 27–8,
    30, 49–51
Potts, Maff, 47–9
poverty, 95–6
    and children and families social
        work, 97
    children living in, 96, 97
    impact on children and
        families, 97
    impact on parents, 97
    radical hope, 100
    radical roots, 99
    relational radicals, 100–1
    support through social
        work, 98
    systemic injustice of, 100
    in the UK, 96
Poverty Profile, 96
Poverty-Aware Paradigm for Child
    Protection, 100
Poverty-Aware Social Work
    Paradigm, 100
power relations, 117–19, *see also*
    supervision
presenteeism, 138
prisoners, 78–9
Professional Standards for Social
    Work in England, 87

professional trust and autonomy, 141
purposeful person-centred
    approach, 27–8, 30

racism. *See* anti-racist leadership;
    anti-racist supervision
Range, Sarah
    core memories, 8
    early life, 10
    and the pantry (university
        programme), 10–11
    as a practitioner, 11–12
    preparation for her turn,
        9–10
reciprocity, and relationships,
    40–1
reciprocity imperative, 39
reflection, 30, 31
relationship-based practice,
    23–4, 32
    EMPOWER model . *See*
        EMPOWER model
    meaning of, 24
    significance of, 25
relationships, 1, 7
    and core memories, 8
    importance of, 11–12
    keys to connections and
        solutions, 12–13
    patchwork of, 7–8
    professional relationship
        limitations, 13
    reflections, 14
    and Strengths approach, 37–8
    and sustainability, 90
    and vulnerability, 39
    and well-being, 140

Relationships and Reciprocity
    model, 40–1
resilience, 34, 39
    through interaction, 140–1
    and supervision, 141
restorative approach, 29–30, 31
risk, and safeguarding, 46
roles, of PSW, 1–2

safeguarding, 45–6, 52
    and Camerados, 47–9
    community-based, 51–2
    jargon, 46–7
    and neighbour, 49–51
    and risk, 46
school uniform grant, 98
Series of Conversations, 105–7, 109
shared social attitudes, 122
Signs of Safety practice
    framework, 110
Social Care Futures, 71
Social Care Workplace Race
    Equality Standards
    (SCWRES), 116
Social Graces, 103
social media, 55, 56, 57
Social Work England, 87, 91, 131
Standards for Employers of Social
    Workers in England, 131
status, in cyberspace, 62–3
story-telling, digital, 58
strengths-based approach, 33, 41, 72
    authentic connection and
        collaboration, 39
    and Care Act 2014, 35
    and community strengths-based
        models, 37

complexity of, 36
effectiveness of, 35
meaning of, 33–5
and personal contribution, 39
and personal needs, 39
principles of, 34–5
problems with, 36
and relational vulnerability, 39
and relationship, 37–8
Relationships and Reciprocity
    model, 40–1
strengths-based community-led
    support, 37, 52
stress, 141
due to social work, 139–40
racial, 124–5
superficiality, accusation of, 34
supervision, 14, 115
and anti-racism policy and
    practice, 116–17
anti-racist practice in, 125–6
and CPD, 132
and micro-aggression, 122–4
probable behaviours and their
    impacts, 119–21
race and power relations
    in, 117–19
race, racism and behaviours
    in, 119
racial stress and trauma, 124–5
and racism, 121–2
and resilience, 141
sustainability, 83–4
and co-creation, 89
concerns, 90–1
and easiness, 88
and individual behaviour
    change, 86–7

meaning of, 84–5
and money, 88–9
and relationships, 90
and social work, 91–2
understanding of, 85–6
and values, 87
SWE Professional Standards for
    Social Work Education, 87
sympathy, 26

TACT Fostering and Adoption
    guidance, 15–16
tax rebates, 98
toxic disinhibition, of online
    activities, 60
trauma aware approach, 72
trauma, racial, 124–5
trust, 12

unconscious actions and behaviours,
    and racism, 108

values, and sustainability, 87
visibility, of racism, 111
vision for social work, 144
visualisation, for well-being, 142
vulnerability, 47

Watters, Dominic, 99
Ways of Writing approach, 16, 21,
    see also writing
well-being, 137–8
    activities, 143
    emotional intelligence, 140
    networks of supportive
        relationships, 142
    practices to support, 141–3

well-being (*Continued*)
    professional trust and
        autonomy, 141
    resilience through
        interaction, 140–1
    and stress, 139–40
    understanding, 138–9
Well-being Champions, 142
whole-system approach,
    28, 31
Wiltshire Local Authority, 16
workplace behaviours, 67
writing, 15–16
    and attention, 21

avoiding generalisations in, 17
capturing narratives, 18
celebrating success, 18
clarity and facts, 17
about concerns, 19–20
consistency in, 20–1
describing complex
    emotions, 17
with empathy, sensitivity and
    respect, 18
engagement of children
    in, 18
including names in, 16
sensitivity in, 19, 21